Wisdom for Millennials and Others

Frank Perroni

ISBN 978-1-63961-158-4 (paperback)
ISBN 978-1-63961-159-1 (digital)

Christian Faith Publishing
832 Park Avenue
Meadville, PA 16335
www.christianfaithpublishing.com

Illustrations by Deanna Yildez, Freelance Artist
deanna@sunnysidestudios.com

Printed in the United States of America

I am beyond grateful for all the effective help of my parents; teachers; schoolmates; friends; and extraordinary helpmate, my dear wife, Norma; sons Joe and Lucas; granddaughter, Jessica; and so many good people like my employers and customers, who were also my tutors.

Author's Introduction

Everyone desires success. For some, that is security. For others, it is comfort or love, or accomplishments. Wealth may provide some help in reaching these goals, and here is a story to illustrate acquiring success, wealth, and all that goes along to make life happy.

A Story

In a high mountain country, a traveler was lost in a snowstorm and could not survive the night without finding shelter. Fortunately, he came upon a rescue cabin with all the provisions which he could need. Inside the sturdy cabin were food, a cast-iron stove, kindling, paper, wood, and matches along with cooking pans and food in a small pantry. The man read the instructions, *Traveler, take comfort as you warm yourself, eat, and wait out any storm.* Problem solved! But the traveler was so cold that he stood frozen with fatigue and confusion. He thought, *Stove, give me some heat.* But until he built a fire, the iron stove remained just cold metal, and it seemed to say to him in reply, "Give me some fire, and then I will give you some heat."

And that was what saved the traveler. He warmed his hands, built the fire, cooked a meal, and in the morning, made his way to a town where he paid for supplies to restock the cabin for the next lost soul.

Our Story

In our lifetime, there will be many times when we wish for some rescue or good fortune to provide some safety, comfort, love, or accomplishment. But like the traveler, we will have to build our own "fire" to survive. Wishes without actions are like smoke rings, pretty but disappearing in seconds.

Author's Foreword

From Facts to Knowledge to Understanding
to Realization and onto Wisdom

Knowledge brings power; activated power from knowledge brings success. These days, many pieces of information are available from our phones and tablets. They do not make us smart; they are like bricks awaiting mortar, arrangement, alignment, and curing to form a structure like the walls of a house, an office, or a place of worship.

To continue the simile, pieces of information and facts have to be sorted and tested to become a part of our knowledge or intellectual baseline.

Then to be connected, as bricks are by mortar, we must allow our knowledge to "cure" in order to be transformed into understanding. We test our knowledge, the baseline, to see if it is straight, strong, and fulfills its purpose like a well setup brick and mortar wall that will support the next level of a house.

So far, we have moved from facts to connecting them and gaining knowledge, and then retesting it all so that we possess understanding. It is similar to gaining a driver's license to operate a manual transmission auto or truck. We go from hearing that you have to start the vehicle to putting it into gear.

At first, we think the information makes us smart. As we go from facts—like key, gear shifter, gas pedal, clutch pedal (what's that little third pedal for anyway?)—well, it fits into a new place in our tree of knowledge and understanding. And then we learn that before the vehicle moves, you have to depress the clutch pedal and *then* move the shifter lever into the first position to get started.

So we accept that the coordinated movements of hands and feet will bring us to the stage where we confirm what our instructor is telling us—information comes before knowledge, and then what follows is an understanding of the process. We can now drive the vehicle. But there's more. We have to be coached on how to move carefully, avoid damaging the other cars or running into people nearby. This brings us to the next stage of enlightenment.

This means that we are about to possess realization or a deeper integration of what we have learned. Here we achieve an integration on a physical, emotional, and intellectual level beyond facts, knowledge, and understanding. We enjoy our possession of an awareness, which is even deeper than understanding. We must go through stages of unconscious incompetence to conscious incompetence and progress to conscious competence. This is the possession of a skill.

More valuable still is the next stage in this progression. Once the skill is performed almost automatically, the mind is free to move gracefully to operating on a higher level of wisdom, an unconscious competence. And when we choose to use our skills for good, holding a job and supporting a family, we then use our skill sets ethically and can share the benefits of the job and teaching the skills to others to help them improve their lives. True wisdom means continuously doing good and avoiding evil.

The Bible's book of Proverbs records the words of King Solomon. He first exhorts us to be wise. And how? "The first step is to trust and reverence the Lord." Accepting our place in creation and learning from God's counsel and the lessons of our parents and good teachers are the right path to becoming wise and sharing that wisdom. In doing so, one may become a leader and then helps others reach wisdom.

This list of 365 proverbs and sayings—some religious, many secular—is provided to help us grow in many ways. Please enjoy, practice their counsel, and share with family and friends.

365 Days of the Year—Proverbs, Sayings, Observations, Insights, and Reminders!

January 1
Life's Journey

> *A journey of a thousand miles begins with a single step.*

> (Chinese proverb)

As the new year begins, your plans, resolutions, and timing await a beginning. If you would start today to change or initiate some new activity, then why not take that essential first step?

January 2
Nothing like the Present

Why put off until tomorrow what you can do today?

(Anon)

So it is day 2 of this new year. And what you planned to do yesterday should now be checked off as "done." If not, reflect on the saying, "If you can't find time to do it right, you will have to *make* time to do it over."

January 3
Positive Action

Another day on the 365 days of each year or 366 in the occasional leap year. Did you procrastinate or fulfill your previous action steps?

Procrastinate is from the Latin *procrastina*, which means deferring work until tomorrow or some future time.

A saying comes to mind:

> *There are seven days in the week: Sunday, Monday, Tuesday, Wednesday, Thursday, Friday, and Saturday. But "someday" never seems to come around. If work or changes are deferred to "someday," I will do X, Y, or Z. The chances are good that they will seldom be accomplished.*

January 4
Patience

Rome was not built in a day.

As with all great cities, a house, a building, a palace, or a bridge, the work begins with a plan, gathering resources, assembling the craftsmen, paying for the materials and labor, and seeing the project through to completion.

Is your plan for this year on track?

January 5
The Power of the Mind

Earl Nightingale, the great motivational expert, found a secret wisdom:

We become, what we think about.

It's puzzling at first because it seems like magic or a fantastical formula. Why then are most people *not* rich, thin, athletic, and benevolent? Perhaps it is because they are not thinking about their goal in terms of effective steps to that desired outcome and are not persevering in pursuit of it.

To reframe his discovery, we might say, "We become what we envision only if we concentrate our minds, make a plan, and then follow through on doing the hard work of becoming our more accomplished selves."

January 6
A Key to Success

It's your attitude, not your aptitude, that determines your altitude.

(Zig Ziglar)

An author, Zig Zigler, compressed a lot into these words. A positive "can-do" frame of mind leads to finding solutions to problems and the path to success. By saying, "I can't, I will not, I don't know how to," you are refusing to even *try* to find that path.

January 7
Starting Off

Well begun is half done.

(Anon)

When we take up our work promptly and diligently, the task seems to unfold easily and lead us to a successful conclusion almost without friction or stumbling.

Has the first week of this year reflected your efforts to start promptly and continue on diligently? Are you "in the zone" or stuck in the mud?

January 8
Recovery

Time heals all wounds.

(Anon)

As you go forward into this year, you may grieve about some mistakes or heartfelt losses. In love or in business, within friendships and families, there are many missteps which can leave great pain and frustration. Going forward means learning from our mistakes, forgiving ourselves, and forgiving those who may have hurt us. These steps enable the "cuts" to heal and form the strengthened tissue which heals up stronger than before. Allow time and forgiveness to heal you and move forward.

January 9
Kindness Counts

A mild reply turns away anger.

(Holy Bible)

Our brains are wired for defense, and so we are quick to respond to perceive insults or attacks. The amygdala in our brains prompts a "fight" response so we counterattack angry words or gestures. But the Bible counsels us to respond with a mild reply and to diffuse the aggressive behavior of another. Whether from a stranger, a neighbor, or a family member, this course of action will bring you closer, not farther apart.

January 10
Healthy Routines

Early to bed, early to rise, makes a man happy, healthy, and wise.

(Anon)

In addition to attitude and kindness, a set of good habits can contribute to joy, good health, and wisdom. The discipline of setting a sensible bedtime and early time to awake and get out of bed will go a long way to establishing happiness, a balance of work and healthy lifestyle, and so beyond understanding, gaining a sense of wisdom.

January 11
Explore Nature

An early morning walk is a blessing for the whole day.

(Henry David Thoreau)

To follow up on the sensible time for rest and activity, a walk or other moderate exercise routine triggers the mind, revs up the heart, and even inspires the soul.

January 12
Genuine Magic

Imagination is the true magic carpet.

(Norman Vincent Peale)

Before we begin our day's work, it would be good to envision what you desire to do, how to carry it out successfully, and share the benefits of your accomplishments with family and friends. A "magic flying carpet" existed only in an exotic story, but the real power to transport us to accomplishments begins in the creative imagination. As a wise teacher once said, "One of the most powerful forces in the world is the creative imagination."

January 13
Creativity

First comes thought, then organization of that thought into ideas and plans. Then comes transformation of those plans into reality. The beginning, as you will observe, is in your imagination.

(Napoleon Hill, author)

Again, success is the result of the process, beginning with thought and transformed by imagination of what is possible and the willingness to pursue the work of accomplishing that goal.

January 14
Solutions to Problems!

Leaders think and talk about the solutions. Followers think and talk about the problems.

(Brian Tracy, Canadian American
author and motivator)

You might have heard the advice, "Don't bring up a problem without a suggestion for a solution." Who complains? Usually, the folks who don't have much to offer as a remedy for something which inconveniences or disrupts our lives.

January 15
Imagination Meets Perseverance

What the mind of man can conceive of and believe in, he can achieve.

(Napoleon Hill)

Again, the thought may be "father to the deed," but the conception must be brought to life by planning practically how to reach that goal and following up with persevering hard work.

January 16
Diligence

Nature cannot be tricked or cheated. She will give up to you the object of your struggles only after you have paid her price.

(Napoleon Hill)

As, noted before, accomplishing a goal requires consistent hard work. Life or nature will allow no shortcuts in this equation.

January 17
Opportunities

As one door closes, another opens.

(Alexander Graham Bell)

On your way to success, a roadblock may interrupt your progress. And then it is time to discover another path. As the inventor of our telephone puts it, there is always an alternative method or opening to your goal. Look for it and find it.

January 18
Efficiency

> *As you face any important task, find the time to do it right, or you will have to make time to do it over again.*

> (Anon)

As hurried as you feel and overwhelmed by multiple obligations, your priority must be to do what is before you in a careful and thoughtful way. Good execution of each task leads to calm and preserves time for the other tasks ahead of you.

January 19
Time Is Precious

> *The most precious resource we have is time.*

> (Steve Jobs)

Time is equally distributed. Each of us has twenty-four hours in a day. This means that good use of time relates to efficiency and success in work and human relationships. With wise apportioning of work time, family time, prayer time, exercise, and sleep time, we thrive.

January 20
Discovery

Action expresses priorities.

(Mahatma Gandhi)

If we keep a journal or review of our actions over time, we may recognize what are the things, people, and concerns which we put foremost in our lives. Setting or resetting priorities may provide tremendous "course corrections" as we travel life's road.

January 21
Big Goals

True independence and freedom can only exist in doing what's right.

(Brigham Young, religious leader)

A leader of many, Brigham Young offers us this guide to what we all hope to achieve. It is up to us to ponder and follow this general principle.

January 22
Value

Try not to become a man of success but a man of value.

(Albert Einstein)

Doing what's right, as Brigham Young counsels, brings independence and freedom but also liberates us to contribute to our fellow human beings. We can aim to add value to our world or let it be.

January 23
Strategy

We can do no great things, only small things with great love.

(Mother Teresa, founder of a religious order and canonized saint)

What everyone wants to do is often expressed as "I want to make a difference." Recognizing this, we say the world is not completely "right" as we see it, and so we want to make improvements. Mother (Saint) Teresa counsels to do what you can but with great love.

January 24
Giving and Getting

The miracle is this—the more we share, the more we have.

(Leonard Nimoy)

This "irony" twists the mind's perceptions, but when its grip is released, new understanding replaces discomfort. As we find here, it goes against our intuition that we may gain by dividing our possessions. But rewards come in complex ways. As a candle flame lights many other candles, without its own flame being diminished, the darkness can be dispelled (from actual experience of the 1965 blackout and a successful rescue of some of the eight hundred thousand stranded subway commuters in the first New York City power blackout).

January 25
Problem or Opportunity?

A problem is a chance for you to do your best.

(Duke Ellington, musician)

Each day presents tasks and likely stumbling blocks to our accomplishments. However, each problem holds a potential opportunity to unravel or disclose the hidden value of that obstacle.

Cold, darkness, hunger, disease—all these challenged those who came before our time, but the inventive, creative minds of inventors, builders, researchers, and doctors unlocked the hidden solutions to give us warmth, light, abundant food, and conquests over most diseases. A problem does not immediately equal solution, but reverse engineering a problem can lead to a solution. Ask, "What would it take to ameliorate, arrest, or eliminate this problem?" Put your creative imagination to work on that and believe that *you* can do it.

January 26
Fear Leads to Paralysis

Never let fear of "striking out" get in your way.

(Babe Ruth, home run king)

Fear of failure? Who has not felt that dread facing a difficult task, talk, new relationship, or job? Babe Ruth had talent, great coaching, and a fire inside him which took him, in his time, to the top of professional baseball. Envision your task succeeding your accomplishment as fulfilling, and you will find the mentors, coaches, books, courses, or other support you require. No one builds a bridge alone but with humility and a good heart. You can recruit the helpers who will be your guide to success.

January 27
Climbing the Mountain

Help me help you to climb the mountain.

(Anon)

Inscribed on a wall at the Canadian World's Fair Exhibition in Montreal, Canada, these words explain the task of the guide. Here he urges the novice to become cooperative as they linked together in the ascent of a mountain that they must take careful steps and learn from the guide who has mastered the exercise of ascending to the heights and returning back down safely. Like Babe Ruth, be humble and learn the ways to succeed. Then be like Ruth, who in turn, coached his teammate, Lou Gehrig, to become a "baseball great" by passing along your wisdom to others whenever you can.

January 28
Continuity

The reward for work well done is the opportunity to do more.

(Jonas Salk, MD)

Dr. Salk was a medical doctor, researcher, and crusader against polio. He is credited with the development of the first effective polio vaccine and crusading for its widespread use. In your lifetime, with hard work, you will become successful. And then what? Will you hunger for praise and acquiring material things? Or will you have the fire of a Dr. Salk and the intensity of a Babe Ruth who were not content to capture a title and earn financial security? As the doctor implies, one of the best rewards is that shining opportunity just ahead of you to do "that more" which will multiply your happiness.

January 29
Presence

Presence is more than just being there.

(Malcom Forbes, investor, founder,
and editor of *Forbes* magazine)

One of the greatest gifts you can give is your attentive presence to your spouse, child, relatives, and friends. Also, in the collegiality of business of being part of a team, your "wide awake presence" to the other is not just a courtesy but an intense awareness of who the other person is, wants, needs, or simply must have. This leads to a complete understanding of why you are called upon to contribute of your talent, compassion, or simply to learn what you must do to grow as a student or younger team member in that situation. Puzzled, unsure of how to help? Just be humble, remain "there," and somehow it will become clear.

January 30
Becoming Wise

No man was ever wise by chance.

(Lucius Annaeus Seneca, author)

The Roman philosopher Seneca wrote of many things we must accomplish and worries which we need to avoid. Here he reminds us that to be wise is not the result of luck or coincidence but the result of study, experience, and the humility to learn from others whatever their station in life.

January 31
Pure Love

> *True love begins when nothing is looked for in return.*

(Antoine Saint-Exupéry)

The French author Antoine Saint-Exupéry wrote the book, *The Little Prince*. Some call it a children's book, but it has subtle and wise instructions in how to be generous, respectful, and pure in extending love and devotion to others. As in the quotation above, we might examine our gift of love to family and others we claim to love in light of this balance. Are we just "giving to get," or are we "giving to endow" the ones about whom we care?

Giving without expectation of "getting" is rare. At the end of a month, this could be a healthy check up on how we treat those who are most dear to us.

February 1
Succeeding

Try not to become a man of success but a man of value.

(Albert Einstein)

We admire success. But to succeed, one must first create value. Create value first in oneself, then in helping others to succeed. Foster and nurture yourself and your talents so you can help your spouse, children, colleagues at work, and your community. Self-development becomes the foundation of personal and communal value.

February 2
Realism and Overconfidence

Nemo dat quod non habet.

(No one can give that which he does
not possess.) (Latin proverb)

We would not board an airplane without an experienced pilot at the controls. It seems straightforward. But at times, don't we try to direct, assist, or even force our help on others even when we do not have the required ability to guide them properly? Anyone—partner, parent, priest, or painter—who thinks he knows everything does not imitate what Socrates said out of modesty: "I know that I know nothing." Overstated? Yes, but he had something there.

Overconfidence

You don't know what you don't know.

(Anon)

What is hidden from us is much that we are not aware of. And if we get a gut feeling that we are over our heads, out of our depth, or about to get "lost," it might be time to stop and reorient ourselves. Let's repeat, and let's expand on the saying: "You don't know what you *don't* know, and *that* will come back to hurt you." It may be wise to follow Socrates, the Greek philosopher, who cautioned us against overconfidence, reminding ourselves, "I may know little to nothing about what I am saying or about to do."

February 3
Opportune Moments and
Quality versus Quantity

Time and tide wait for no man.

(Geoffrey Chaucer, medieval poet)

Beware overconfidence, but do not become paralyzed by timidity. There is a time for action whether individual or by team cooperation. When the right moment for action appears, one must go forward.

Quality over Quantity

> *It is not the length of life but the depth.*
> (Ralph Waldo Emerson, poet)

We pray, "God, please give us time to make our beneficial mark on the world. But for some life is shortened, and so we must strive to live "days of quality," as our commitment to making our world better before we leave this life.

February 4
Realism

> *Learn from yesterday, live for today, hope for tomorrow.*

(Albert Einstein)

Each night before bedtime, take stock of what you accomplished in the near yesterday. Think about where it might lead your actions tomorrow. This practice stores lessons learned and prompts strategies for the next day. Usually, it promotes a restful sleep and provides a "game plan" when you wake up the next morning.

February 5
Integrity

> *It takes twenty years to build a reputation and five minutes to destroy it.*

(Warren Buffet, investor)

So much of our value resides in our personal actions, fulfilling our commitments, and collaborating honestly with family, friends, and colleagues. When we live our days with consistent steps on the straight path, guided by the Ten Commandments and other moral guidelines, we maintain our integrity. A solid and good person, who can be trusted and depended upon, is a man or woman of integrity.

("Count no man happy until he dies free of pain at last." Sophocles dramatically commented on this matter with that stark warning. Accordingly, one must live a lifetime of integrity to enjoy an unblemished reputation.)

February 6
Initiative

People of accomplishment rarely sit back and let things happen to them. They go out and make things happen.

(Leonardo da Vinci, inventor and artist)

Five centuries before there were airplanes, helicopters, and submarines, there were visions of these marvels, diagramed by a thinker and inventor, Leonardo da Vinci. His visions awaited fulfillment via the combustion engine and computer-guided construction. But he pushed our imaginations to fly, hover, and travel beneath the oceans.

February 7
Results

Whatever one sows, That, he will also reap. (Jacob 4:8)

This is a profound principle which reminds us of the equilibrium between our efforts we put in and the end products of our labors. Given good seeds with adequate soil and climate, a proportionate harvest of wheat will come in due season. Sow what is good to expect a good to an excellent result.

February 8
Proportionality

Sow seeds of doubt and expect insecurity, but sow seeds of hope and expect optimism.

(Max Lucado, author)

As discussed, our attitude is critical to our rate of success in life. Why put into our minds thoughts of insecurity and failure when we could implant thoughts of hope and future success?

February 9
Tenacity

What isn't tried won't work.

(Claude MacDonald, motivator)

How can I improve something? This or that might be too extreme or risky, but without trying it or some scaled-down variation of that tactic, a solution may escape our grasp.

February 10
Hate versus Love—a Remedy

> *Darkness cannot drive out darkness; only light can do*
> *that. Hate cannot drive out hate; only love can do that.*

(Martin Luther King Jr., pastor)

Emotions are real and may rule us if we allow them to do so. But our emotions can be ruled and replaced when they lead us to break the social compact with our neighbors. Hate is a very corrosive force. Externalized, it hurts others. And when internalized, it consumes and destroys ourselves. As Dr. King advises, "love others" so that we find harmony and peace with one another.

February 11
Commerce

Price is what you pay. Value is what you get.

(Warren Buffett, investor)

Ordinarily, a "price" implies sacrifice or pain. Sometimes the transaction of payment for a product or service creates regret, and at other times, pleasure. When a customer looks at a steep price for equipment, such as a home or a car, the expectations are daunting. Realize that for an exchange of treasure, the product should be weighed in terms of value and quality to be received over time. Are you just buying a house or providing a family with a home for all that money? It will make a great deal of difference over time.

February 12
Feelings—Deep Impressions

*People will forget what you said and forget what you
did but never forget how you made them feel.*

(Maya Angelou, poet, civil rights activist)

Someone asked me, "What is classy?" I took that to mean kind or considerate, and I replied, "Treat everyone with respect, and make them feel important." Maya Angelou put it well, that the lasting impressions we make on others reside in how they feel after your interaction with them. We can say or do something healing or hurtful, informative or inspiring. What they come away with is a powerful impression of what happened to them more than who you were or what you wore. Did you impart respect and importance to this soul? Well done.

February 13
Opportunities

Opportunities are usually disguised as hard work, so most people don't recognize them.

(Ann Landers, columnist)

Sounds repulsive, yes? Here's some hard work facing you today, and it has to be done today and done well. What a challenge! We shrink from our hardest tasks and look around for other things to do or ways to procrastinate, sending those prickly things further off to another day on our calendars. Two suggestions: Start with a short light task, utilizing that one as a warm-up for the bigger chore. Recognize the value of completing the big chore and divide it into component parts to analyze the required solutions. Then piece the parts together to form the finished job. Doing the "hard job" may uncover your own hidden talents or direct you onto a new path to success.

February 14
Immediately—Daunting Words

Go now; procrastinate later.

(Vince Poscente, author, business consultant)

When an action now, and not later, is required, imperative and unavoidable, it is preferable to do *it* and get it accomplished. Why not do what you need to do now, not later, not a part of it, and likely leave the other part undone? Sounds ridiculous when you lay it out like this, so why not employ the old 1-2-3—start, continue, finish.

February 15
The Grade of Incomplete

It's the job that's never started that takes longest to finish.

(J. R. R. Tolkien, author of *The Hobbit*)

Look at your list of priorities and ask which tasks are listed top to bottom and find out how many are incomplete, overlooked, half began, or totally neglected. What happened? What needs to happen?

49

February 16
Heroism through Selflessness

True heroism is not the urge to surpass all others at whatever the cost but the urge to serve others at whatever the cost.

(Arthur Ashe, champion tennis player)

Wanting to get ahead? Surely everyone wants to exceed and surpass high expectations at their job or hobby. Arthur Ashe was a wise man who succeeded by thinking of and serving others. While he became a champion at tennis, he also coached younger players becoming a role model so they could follow in his steps to their own championships.

February 17
Wisdom, a Gift to be Shared

Wisdom is the power to put our time and our knowledge to the proper use.

(Thomas J. Watson, businessman
and former chairman of IBM)

Knowledge is power, but understanding comes next. And when it is internalized into deeper realizations, it is opportune and right to share that, which is your wisdom.

February 18
Perseverance, a Long, Hard Road

If you can dream it, you can do it.

(Walt Disney, founder of the Disney
entertainment empire)

Walt Disney tells a simple truth. If you can imagine something you desire to create, you can do it. He was able to transform his dream into a reality by his effort, pains, and unending persistence. If your dream is grand, expect to take a long and hard road trip to "Successville."

February 19
A Vision

> *I saw the angel in the marble, and I carved until I*
> *set him free.*

(Michelangelo, master sculptor and artist)

A vision requires concomitant effort to be born. The form which this great artist and sculptor imagined could come forth from a simple block of stone, required skill and patience, trial and refinement. The statue, which takes our breath away, took thousands of breaths and thousands of strokes to free the angel from the stone. Persistence, skill, and labor bring forth beauty.

February 20
Valor—a Critical Element

Nature has placed nothing so high that it is out of the reach of industry and valor.

(Alexander the Great, ancient
king and empire builder)

Valor means courage, which comes from the heart. How much can be accomplished if one exerts the effort from the heart?

February 21
Generosity—Essential to Life

The most satisfying thing in life is to have been able to give a large part of one's self to others.

(Teilhard de Chardin, priest and poet)

We look out at the world through our own eyes, and so it is hard to see the world through the eyes of others. As we would want others to understand and love us, it is first through the giving of one's self that we receive understanding and commensurate love in return.

February 22
Heartfelt, a Wise Assessor

> *The best and most beautiful things in the world*
> *cannot be seen or even touched—they must be felt*
> *with the heart.*

(Helen Keller, blind student and wise teacher)

Most things we value are measured by weight, size, brightness, or other physical aspects. Helen Keller had no eyesight, but she had "heart sight" or the ability to know a person's value or the measure of their gifts by weighing them in her heart.

February 23
Contemplation: Quietude or
Music—They Both Teach

*After silence, that which comes nearest to expressing
the inexpressible, is music.*

(Aldous Huxley, novelist)

Silence is difficult to attain for any length of time, but it stirs thought. Music, especially structured and at slow tempo like sections of a concerto or symphony, arrests the flighty mind and allows deeper thoughts and emotions to find their places in our hearts like books well arranged on a shelf.

February 24
Tenderness—a Priceless Quality

A mother's arms are made of tenderness, and children sleep soundly in them.

(Victor Hugo, author)

A newborn infant in a mother's arms is a picture to behold. As the infant grows, the mother's embrace becomes more welcomed and acknowledged but never rejected. Tenderness should be expressed by dads and siblings as well. A little tenderness is not weakness but a powerful strength given outward and restoring to the giver simultaneously.

February 25
Examples—Better than Words

My father didn't tell me how to live; he lived, and let me watch him do it.

(Clarence Budington Kelland, American author)

When we learn things and absorb ethical principles, we hear words and observe actions. In the family setting, it is most likely that we learn and practice the actions and attitudes of our parents faster and more deeply from their actions than their words.

February 26
Peace—Essential to Life

> *My films must let every man, woman, and child know that God loves them, that I love them, and peace and salvation will become a reality only when they learn to love each other.*
>
> (Frank Capra, filmmaker and director of *It's a Wonderful Life*)

Frank Capra made touching films with a purpose which echoed his deep belief. We all create a story by way of our own lives, so consider whether or not our lifetime drama is a positive contribution to this goal of true peace.

February 27
Acts—Actions Affect Outcomes

Small acts, when multiplied by millions of people,
can transform the world.

(Howard Zinn, American historian)

If multiplied actions cause magnified results, we should align our actions for good.

February 28,
Success, a Goal, or a Process?

> *Success is not the key to happiness. Happiness is the key to success. If you love what you are doing, you will be successful.*

(Albert Schweitzer, doctor, missionary, and theologian)

A man of science and devoted to helping the needy surprises us by his ironic view of success, which brings what? In his view, your work and the pleasure you bring to others provide for your own pleasure and a sense of worth. Success equals joyfully giving something valuable to others throughout your lifetime.

March 1
Significance—Weighed in the Relationship

To the world, you might be one person, but to one person, you might be the world.

(Anonymous)

Are you one of many? Or are you "the one" out of many who makes life significant for another? Sometimes we may feel lost or unnoticed by the many people in our group at school or work, but look at who is looking up *to* you. Your life may be the focus of that other person. Are not gratitude and reciprocal focus appropriate?

March 2
Gentleness—Emotional Medicine

Gentleness corrects whatever is offensive in our manner.

(Hugh Blair, Scottish minister and professor)

What is a gentleman or gentlewoman but one who exhibits moderation, kindness, and caring. Let our manner be gentle.

March 3
Discovery—Sometimes an Internal Revelation

Look well into thyself; there is a source of strength which will always spring up, if thou will always look there.

(Marcus Aurelius, Roman emperor
and stoic philosopher)

Energy on demand! From gasoline, abundant electricity, the morning cup of coffee to vitamins, we look outward for strength and power to fuel our cars, our homes, and bodies. Where do we find the psychic energy demanded by stressful relationships, overwhelming tasks, and demanding changes in our lives? The stoic philosopher of Ancient Rome said simply look deep within. As he directed, look "deep within" yourself to perceive that inner source of strength.

March 4
Different but Respectful

We confide in our strength without boasting of it;
we respect that of others without fearing it.

(Thomas Jefferson, third president of the USA)

There will never be equality of talents and treasures possessed by human beings. The peacemaker among these disparities will accept this situation with humility and respects each one's gifts as composing a part of the totality of human accomplishment. The bricklayer is not a surgeon, but each must acknowledge the talent of the other.

March 5
Trust Essential to Progress

Loyalty and devotion lead to bravery. Bravery leads to the spirit of self-sacrifice. The spirit of self-sacrifice creates trust in power of love.

(Morihei Ueshiba, founder of the school
of Aikido, the "gentle self-defense art")

Master Ueshiba created a "way," a philosophy of peaceful harmonious interaction with the world and other persons. His nonviolent self-defense art, Aikido, stems from his belief that the world is harmonious, and we should act in accordance with that. Do not hit an attacker but subdue him.

March 6
Struggle—Ironically, a Building Force

There is no life without struggle.

(Santosh Kalwar, author)

Are we lazy by nature, or are we in search of accomplishment without pain? We may find that accomplishment is born out of some amount of struggle. Does a concept make money? Not at first, or sometimes not even when it is built out into a product or service. With continued work and refinement, success comes along.

March 7
Who Are You?—It's Not What
Others "Think" of You

Those people who hate you envy your freedom.

(Santosh Kalwar, author)

Do you feel dejected because others show you no respect or acceptance? Sometimes our different ways reflect our independence and striving for goals, which are out of the reach or efforts of others. Perhaps they "envy" your freedom. Take it as a mark of honor, not shame or enmity.

March 8
Time—a Precious Commodity

I must govern the clock, not be governed by it.

(Golda Meir, former prime minister of Israel)

The workday, homelife, vacations, or just restful restorative naps all demand a portion of our time. Prime minister or household engineer? Whatever our vocation, today we hear the exhortation, "Have a work-life balance." It presents a guideline to balanced behavior, which we can embrace, reject, or personalize.

March 9
Flexibility, a Valuable Trait

Expect the best. Prepare for the worst. Capitalize on what comes.

(Zig Ziglar, author)

When approaching a critical future point, Zig Zigler offers three options. This implies positive attitude, strength of character, and flexibility to manage any one of the three outcomes which come along. Being positive prepares us for success, but when the worst event arises, be strong, and finally, do what makes a good or terrible outcome even better. Flexibility helps in sports, in relationships, and in business. You expect it from champions and want it in our family and friends. Why not practice it yourself?

March 10
Relationships—What and with Whom?

Relationship is about forgiveness and compromise. It is about balance where one person complements each other.

(Nicholas Sparks, novelist)

From infancy to old age, we begin, foster, and grow our attachments to others. Ideally, all these interactions are positive, but the most enduring ones are balanced and, as Nicholas Sparks identifies, are mutually helpful to compete the other person. Child to parent, spouse to spouse, parent to children, and then grandchildren, the road of great relationships is extensive and challenging.

March 11
The Magic of Math

Happiness adds and multiplies as we divide it with others.

(A. Nielsen)

A shared attitude can be productive or reductive; it depends on the attitude. We divide our griefs when we share our pains with supportive friends and can uplift them by sharing our happiness. Candor and trust, communication and active listening facilitate this process. Think back on how a friend uplifted you or you turned someone's sadness around. Some gifts cost no money, only effort. And truly caring and sharing, reward both the receiver and the giver.

March 12
Partners

Friendship is essentially a partnership.

(Aristotle, philosopher)

Aristotle praises genuine friendship, which is a shared, mutually helpful relationship. He extols this partnership by further stating, "Without friends, no one would want to live even if he had all the other goods."

And he cautions that "wishing to be friends is quick work, but friendship is a slow ripening fruit." Putting it all together, you see that living well requires friends who, over time, prove they can trust deeply and truly care for each other's well-being.

March 13
Gratitude—Maintaining Your Blessings

Hem your blessing with thankfulness so they don't unravel.

A hem or strong border on a garment prevents tears, which can undo the integrity of your clothes. As mentioned to us when children, "say thank you" when someone gives you a gift or does you a favor. Time's passage may dull the memory of that counsel, but gratitude nurtures kindness and reciprocity. All gifts from family, friends, or blessings from heaven deserve acknowledgment internally and in words.

March 14
The Now and the Then

When life closes a door, God opens a window.

(Anonymous)

Opportunities come one after another, but at a critical point, they seem to stop. And it seems that life is totally blocking your progress with a closed iron door. Where will the light come from? Just about then, God seems to open a window, a skylight, or create a backdoor to provide your next direction at that time. So it may be a small window—climb out! Is it a backdoor leading in a new direction? Follow it anyway. And above all, be grateful.

March 15
Awe—Available, Free, and Transforming

Be filled with wonder, be touched by peace.

(Anonymous)

Several days out of the week, we may be unhappy, troubled, even depressed. What has the power to darken our spirits is often transitory or resolved with the help of friends, colleagues, or simply nature. When we stop looking down and gaze upward to mountains, treetops, a sunrise, or a church spire, we find *awe* coming on and over us. It diminishes the small, trivial troubles in our lives. Yes, wonder and respect for God's beautiful creations will free us from sadness and provide peace. Peace will help us find our way.

March 16
A Smile—Easy Therapy

Make someone smile whenever you can, you never know how much of a difference you could be making in their life at that moment.

(Anonymous)

If you ever saw the light in someone's eyes brighten up from a gratuitous smile you shared, you will agree with this assessment. But not knowing the nature of the internal battle the other person is fighting, you may assume that your silent communication is unwanted and irrelevant. But your smile might provide low-cost and effective therapy.

March 17
Perseverance—Required Attitude

*You have to fight through some bad days to earn the
best days of your life.*

(Anonymous)

Hard to admit it, but problems come along for our ultimate good. As was said, "Opportunities come along disguised as problems." And as you fight through the dark days, you win the battle of "fight or flight" and persevere to the "win" accomplishing the "goals" which you are seeking. Giving up means defeat. Battling onward brings victory. Winning is always a matter of when, not if.

March 1
Small or Large

Small opportunities are often the beginning of great enterprises.

(Demosthenes, Ancient Greek
statesman and orator)

Foresight brought success to many. They looked at problems, some large, others small, and decided to find solutions. In recent times, these have overcome aggravations, inconveniences, and burdensome activities. Look at air conditioning, automatic transmissions in vehicles, washing machines, computers, and cell phones. Small problems overcome led to massive industries.

March 19
Many or Few—a Balance Required

Wealth consists not in having great possessions but in having few wants.

(Epictetus, Ancient Greek stoic
teacher philosopher)

It is essential to distinguish wants from needs. Our needs are few, such as air, food, shelter, security, companionship, and understanding. But our wants are almost limitless. Epictetus reminds us, "Some things are in our control, and others are not." We are surrounded by so many desirable things, advertised to us as things we must have and disguised as needs when, actually, they are attractive but not essential to our lives. It is best to select what is appropriate for your happiness from the multiplicity of goods you might want.

March 20
Quantity and Quality

Better a little which is well done than a great deal imperfectly.

(Plato, philosopher, teacher, and a
founder of Western thought)

Time, effort, skill, and patience—these go into producing precision instruments and objects from watches to jetliners. What Plato said was paraphrased to our disgruntled group of impatient travelers enduring a delayed flight. "We are correcting a problem on the aircraft, so do you want it done fast or done right?" We were happy to board the airplane two hours later and arrived safely thanks to a job well done.

March 21
Transitions

When I let go of what I am, I become what I might be.

(Lao Tzu, Chinese philosopher and founder of Taoism)

Who am I, and who are you? Questions prompt answers relating to what we do, where we stand in the course of our lives. Mother, father, son or daughter, student or professor? But is that all we are? Lao Tzu reminds us that potential inside of each of us awaits a release. One way to free that potential is to reflect on what we have done and become without seeing that as final. A declaration that "this alone" is our totality, a presumption that we are fixed or at present, "all that we are" locks the door to a bigger world out there.

March 22
Generosity

When you are laboring for others, let it be with the same zeal as if it were for yourself.

(Confucius, Chinese teacher and philosopher)

Pressed by our own needs, struggling to keep our place and advance in a profession? Confucius offers a better perspective when he asks that we view our labor as mutually productive for one another. "Putting your heart into your work transforms simple labor into art."

March 23
Priorities

Dignity does not consist in possessing honors but in deserving them.

(Aristotle, Greek philosopher)

Honors, promotions, degrees, and badges of merit are what we desire. Sometimes they are given before they are truly merited. If you can sleep well with your medals and badges of distinction, then your dignity is well earned. Strive to earn the next levels of success, and wear your title with calm humility.

March 24
Endurance

What you leave behind is not what is engraved in monuments but what is woven into the lives of others.

(Pericles, Ancient Greek statesman)

Do you wonder what you will endow by your actions during a lifetime of labor and human relationships? A wise stateman, Pericles, cautions that your best gift to the world and others may be your enduring influence in their lives.

March 25
Courage

Courage is knowing what not to fear.

(Plato, Greek philosopher)

We admire and want to acquire bravery. When young, we are told to be courageous and conquer our fears so we can win our battles. All good so far, but in a twist, Plato reminds us that courage is also a choice of perceiving when to be brave and when to retreat from overwhelming odds. As it has been said, "Choose your battles, and you may win without a fight."

March 26
Balance

True happiness is to enjoy the present without anxious dependence on the future.

(Seneca, Roman philosopher)

Yesterday, today, and tomorrow—when we live in the past or the future, we may be shortchanging the present. Past accomplishments or losses are behind us and should only be lessons. Don't indulge in vanity or grieving. The future is ahead and must be planned carefully. The present is here and is the ground on which we work. Be present in the now.

March 27
Humility

Neither blame nor praise yourself.

(Plutarch, Greek historian)

A lesson in psychology from centuries ago: Blame is harsh, but accepting responsibility for one's failures is healthy. Praising oneself is vanity in action. As Aristotle cautioned, honors must be merited for the title to be valid. "Dignity consists in earning an honor."

March 28
A Good Man

Waste no time arguing what a good man should be.
Be one.

(Marcus Aurelius, emperor of Rome)

The general and statesman urged us to understand what we are and what we can become. Also he said, "You have power over your mind, not outside events." What you can become and how to live well rest largely upon ourselves and the willingness to reflect on and strive for the best in us.

March 29
Resilience

The oak fought the wind and was broken, the willow bent when it must and survived.

(Robert Jordan, author)

We fight many forces, but when they intend to break us, it is time to be more like the willow than the oak tree. That does not mean surrendering our core values, nor shirking responsibilities, but learning how to bend with excessive stress and not have our will be broken.

March 30
Resolute

You may have to fight a battle more than once to win it.

(Margaret Thatcher, former prime minister of England)

You won, or so you thought. The opposition returns and, with deceit, snatches your victory away, sneaking off and hoping you will not follow to fight again. But a strong person will not concede a victory to falsehood and returns to the battle, and finally wins.

March 31
Strong Foundations

*Rock bottom became the solid foundation in which
I rebuilt my life.*

(J. K. Rowling, modern author)

When we hear he or she has "hit the bottom," we feel sadness and pity. But sometimes that bottom is a barrier which will not be pierced and a floor under our feet on which we stand up and walk onward.

April 1
Looking Forward

Measured against eternity, our time on earth is just a blink of an eye, but the consequences of it will last forever.

(Rick Warren, author, pastor)

To persons of faith, this world is not our lasting existence. Our souls will one day meet the Creator and spend an eternity with Him in bliss or without Him in despair. God's rules are clear, and living by them fulfills our mission to be our best, fulfilling our designed purpose and living on happily after this earthly life is done.

April 2
Gratitude—Essential Virtue

Gratitude is the sign of noble souls.

(Aesop, Greek author)

Gifts are bestowed on us from birth to death. Our parents, teachers, mentors, employers, friends, spouses, and even some antagonistic opponents teach us in so many ways. Be it a compliment or a reprimand, we can take the high road and be grateful or the low road of resentment or a sense of entitlement. How we handle the harsh or the soft strokes of experience shapes us.

April 3
Grateful Persons

Among the things you can give and still keep are your word, a smile, and a grateful heart.

(Zig Ziglar, author, motivational speaker)

An old saying runs, "You can't have your cake and eat it too." But unlike the material elements of cake or candy, our attitudes and good conduct transcend the limits of consumption and depletion. When you keep your word, send and enjoy your rebounding smile and hold onto an attitude of gratitude, you will be the wiser and the richer.

April 4
Taking a Stand

Be sure you put your feet in the right place, then stand firm.

(Abraham Lincoln, president of the United
States in the time of the Civil War)

At times we are called to stand up for what is right and precious. President Lincoln had one of the most difficult jobs in American history. Once he felt the issue was right, he stood firm and guided us through a terrible war to prevent the fatal fracturing of our nation.

April 5
Perduring

Colors fade, temples crumble, empires fall, but wise words endure.

(Edward Thorndike, American psychologist)

From the Bible to proverbs, wise sayings, and sage commentaries, we find gems of wisdom that span the centuries and shine lights on our complex circumstances. These lights clarify what courses of action could bring good or bad results. So before reacting, let's consider the wisdom of commandments, principles of philosophers, and poets which can guide us through these forests.

April 6
Opportunities

Great opportunities may come along once in a lifetime, but small opportunities surround us every day.

(Rick Warren, pastor and author)

Those many opportunities can be packaged as problems or other annoyances, but they all deserve our attention. Why does this trouble us? What if it could be removed or transformed into its opposite? This approach has led to management insights, life-changing inventions, and just plain small improvements in our lifetimes. Turn the problem over and look for what its hidden solution might suggest.

April 7
Action, not Reaction

People of accomplishment rarely sit back and let things happen to them. They go out and make things happen.

(Leonardo da Vinci, artist, inventor)

Beyond acquiring the basics of life and small measures of success, we desire to make a difference or make the world a better place. The gigantic talent of Leonardo da Vinci would be unknown to us if he refused to ponder, discover, and record in drawings his vision of "making the world a better place." He created "blueprints" of the future, sharing his talent with the world of his times.

April 8
Do It—Now

Lost time is never found again.

(Benjamin Franklin, ambassador, inventor, and author)

When you have made that discovery or hit by a breakthrough ideas, it is *the* time to follow through. Order your thoughts, write them down, share them with colleagues, put them through trial-and-error testing to confirm or adjust them so the idea becomes a reality to become a genuine contribution.

April 9
The Now

Do not dwell in the past, do not dream of the future,
concentrate the mind on the present moment.

(Buddha, born Siddhārtha Gautama, philosopher, teacher, and spiritual leader)

Great thoughts from our teachers. Apply them judiciously. If you are tasked with inventing what will cure a disease or make a plane fly more safely, you might disagree with the cautionary note, "Do not dream of the future." But in deepening your assessment of your *now*, you will be able to envision where your search will take you to reach an improved future.

April 10
Honesty

Honesty is the first chapter in the book of wisdom.

(Thomas Jefferson, third president of the USA)

How can I be honest with myself and others? Honesty is being truthful and avoiding exaggerations or self-serving rationalizations. When we bring our real selves to the family table, the workplace, or the marketplace, we offer the value of a trustworthy partner. It is the beginning of solid relationships and moves us to become good and wise persons.

April 11
Change Is Challenging

Taking a new step, uttering a new word, is what people fear most.

(Fyodor Dostoyevsky, author)

New job, new school, new town, new family responsibilities? Whatever the changes which affect our performance and self-image can intimidate us. We become who we expect to be by facing and overcoming these challenges. Being honest about our fears and short-comings can lead us up or down. It is wiser to call for help when we need a mentor or a counselor to succeed.

April 12
Troubles Will Come Along Often

> *Trouble will come along soon enough, and when he does come, receive him as pleasantly as possible. The more amiably you greet him, the sooner he will go away.*

> (Artemus Ward, pen name of Charles Browne, author, humorist)

Personifying "Mr. or Ms. Trouble" as an irksome visitor opens our eyes to perception, masking itself as reality. As we shake hands with this visitor and learn what problems he or she may present, we can cordially set him or her down for a chat. Why do you bother me? Oh, so that's the problem? Well, behind the veil of that disturbance could lie opportunity. So it's best to conduct your interview cordially and discover the hidden value of the visit.

April 13
Wise and Grateful

No one who achieves success does so without acknowledging the help of others. The wise and confident acknowledge this help with gratitude.

(Alfred North Whitehead, mathematician and philosopher)

How can we separate our knowledge from the gift of teachers, books, coaches, mentors, parents, and grandparents who all helped us attain the gift of learning by sharing their learned and earned experiences? They did so much for us that it would be illogical to say we became wise by ourselves and selfish to deny them our gratitude. Everyone desires some acknowledgment for their contributions, and those who elevated us to knowledge and understanding deserve due credit.

April 14
Quality Control

People in their handling of affairs often fail when they are about to succeed. If one remains as careful at the end as he was at the beginning, there will be no failure.

(Lao Tzu, Chinese philosopher)

In every process which aims at quality control of a service or product, the result is most important. Many careful steps in making a product or correct processes in crafting a service are essential to a good outcome. As found in the medical world, another step is called quality assurance. That meant that only excellent materials would be accepted at the head of the production line. We can apply that to our motivations and choice of friends or a field of work. If we start out with the best and perform quality checks all the way through, the outcome will be marked "excellent."

April 15
Success: How to Measure It?

> *Success is to be measured not so much by the position*
> *that one has reached in life as by the obstacles which*
> *he has had to overcome while trying to succeed.*

> (Booker T. Washington, author,
> educator, intellectual)

Born just before the Civil War into slavery, he rose beyond many obstacles to become a leader in education and advised presidents. Our obstacles may seem to be daunting but consider them miniscule beside those who start out in life shackled by enormous burdens. Take up our burdens as future badges of honor to be claimed by succeeding despite their weight.

April 16
Failure Is Not a Good Plan

If you fail to plan, you are planning to fail.

(Benjamin Franklin, inventor and USA ambassador)

A plan is a road map or a sea chart. Without a view of the starting points and destinations, travelers will wander and become lost. Parents tell us to get an education, pastors advise us to follow the commandments, and financial advisors urge us to plan for the days ahead when we will retire from earning our daily living. Benjamin Franklin's advice is currently rephrased as this: "People don't plan to fail, they just *fail* to plan." To be among the 5 percent of well-retired people, we must plan and follow a well-thought-out plan.

April 17
Time Is Limited

Your time is limited, so don't waste it living someone else's life.

(Steve Jobs, inventor, designer, entrepreneur, and cofounder of Apple Computing)

A man of extraordinary talent and drive, Steve Jobs lived to accomplish his visions for better communications. Should we dismiss his thoughts about time and being yourself or make them a part of our strategy for living well?

April 18
Happiness? It's a Shield against Difficulties

Your success and happiness lie in you. Resolve to keep happy, and your joy shall form an invincible host against difficulties.

(Helen Keller, author)

As every day begins, whether with a smile or a frown, your face can set the mood and the pattern for the outcome of the day's battles with difficulties. Are you joyful in the morning, grateful for the chance to help members of your family, friends, coworkers, and neighbors? Overcoming blindness and deafness, Helen Keller could do so. Happiness is your ally in the battle to succeed.

April 19
True Friendship Is a Blessing

The days will pass. Good friends remain.

(Thomas Rifleman, scientist, patriot)

A good friend is the closest thing to an adopted family member. Although you do not share any DNA, you share a bond created by concern, mutual assistance, support, and a shoulder to lean upon. Tom, through his advice and example of maturity, has taught many colleagues and made of them good friends who remain in his care and love. His love of country proved him to be an example for all.

April 20
Love—Quintessentially Required

> *Love is the immortal flow of energy that extends,*
> *nourishes, and preserves. Its eternal goal is life.*

(Smiley Blanton, author, physician, psychiatrist)

Love is mostly equated with emotional attachment or passion. Dr. Blanton reaches us with a deeper reminder that love is a benign force which results in the extension of life itself. So in a sense, love begets devotion. Devotion is the work of protection, service, and selfless care for the ones we are privileged to love.

April 21
The Terrier and the Great Dane

*Things that upset a terrier, may pass virtually unno-
ticed by a Great Dane.*

(Smiley Blanton, author)

Dr. Blanton sets up the comparison between a small dog, the terrier, and one of the largest of the breed of dogs, a Great Dane. One is ruffled by an event which goes by the big dog. Well, the small things tend to bother small creatures but hardly trouble big people. What shall we be, terrier or Great Dane?

April 22
Calm

You can overcome all, if you think you can. Keep your calmness and sense of humor.

(Smiley Blanton, author)

Attitude against problems—like the big dog who shrugs off little annoyances, Dr. Blanton recommends a positive attitude and the grace of a sense of humor as the antidote to pesky problems.

April 23
Key Things

It's not the years in your life that count. It's the life in your years.

(Abraham Lincoln, sixteenth president of the USA, emancipator)

How did a farm boy from Kentucky who struggled for education and political office come to affect the survival of our nation and the end of slavery in the county? He crowded an immense amount of life into his fifty-six short years. Each day begins with hope and expectation. Do we really appreciate the gift of our time here? What else can we accomplish today and within our lifespans?

April 24
The Possible

It is difficult to say what is impossible, for the dream of yesterday is the hope of today and the reality of tomorrow.

(Robert H. Schuller, pastor and evangelist)

Jet flight, moon landings, driverless cars, artificial intelligence guiding doctors' diagnoses, and stem cells regenerating our physical organs were considered dreams or fantasies years ago. Well, the hope of today may be the reality of tomorrow. It's up to all of us to apply our talents to make it happen.

April 25
Pursuit

All things come to those who go after them.

(Rob Estes, American actor)

Why do we wait for things to come to us? Examples of discoveries and serendipity are plentiful but seem to befriend other people. If you want something you perceive to be beneficial to you and not harmful to others, go after it. When you catch up to it, be grateful.

April 26

One loyal friend is worth ten thousand relatives.
(Euripides, Ancient Greek
author and playwright)

It has been said, "You can choose your friends but not your relatives." So the choice of a loyal friend may turn out to be more supportive than many who, by chance, have come to be our relatives. But we can have both: strong loyalty from friends and family members. Remember that friendship requires reciprocal energy from both sides.

April 27
Good Fortune

Luck is a matter of preparation, meeting opportunity.

(Lucius Annaeus Seneca, Roman
author and stoic)

Seneca, the younger, left us a treasury of wise words. This saying may have prompted the motto of actor Rob Estes above. For most of us, it is hard work and preparation, which precede the acquisition of good fortune.

April 28
Time

You will never find time for anything. If you want time, you must make it.

(Charles Buxton, philanthropist and
member of the British parliament)

Mr. Buxton makes a fine point. Time is all around us. But to accomplish what we set out to do, we must not expect the right time to fall into our laps but carve out a period for the work we must do and convert those minutes or hours into plans and actions, which create our desired result.

April 29
Good to Great

Nothing great was ever achieved without enthusiasm.

(Henry Ford, founder of Ford Motors
and inventor of the assembly line)

Passion well directed, excitement about our work, the desire to make something better, sometimes called enthusiasm are essential for producing great products or services. Labor without enthusiasm and you contribute ordinary results. Labor with excitement and a passion for improvement? Likely you will be rewarded well beyond your weekly pay.

April 30
Hit or Miss

Failure is simply an opportunity to begin again.
This time with more intelligence.

(Henry Ford, inventor, business leader)

Failure is not a stop sign. It could be a yield sign signifying a merge or new direction is coming up. Henry Ford did not start his automobile building empire with an assembly line, but he did develop it and improved production and cut costs dramatically. Take the failure as an experiment, a lesson, not a dead end.

May 1
Work Wholeheartedly

Do your work with your whole heart and you will succeed—there's so little competition.

(Elbert Hubbard, American
writer and philosopher)

If you are faced by competition at work or on a team, your short cut to success, as Elbert Hubbard sees it, is wholehearted effort. Suddenly you will become an outstanding performer. He also said, "A machine can do the work of fifty ordinary men. No machine can do the work of one extraordinary man."

May 2
A Better Place

The best way to predict the future is to create it.

(Abraham Lincoln, sixteenth president of the USA)

How often we hear these affirmations, "I want to make this world a better place," or "I want to leave this world in better shape than I found it." Lincoln offered this advice, "To find a better outcome, we must become cocreators. Discover what we have to offer, and then labor wholeheartedly to maximize that talent toward that better place we desire."

May 3
Bravery

The bravest are surely those who have the clearest vision of what is before them, glory and danger alike, and yet, not withstanding, go out to meet it.

(Thucydide, Greek general and historian)

Recognition for bravery comes not from avoiding danger but meeting it head on. The Athenian general from centuries before Christ told us to face and overpower our challenges. We must do the same, whether in wartime or peacetime.

May 4
Problems to Be Solved

Ancient Rome declined because it had a senate. Now what's going to happen to us with both a senate and a house?

(Will Rogers, American actor, writer, humorist)

Will Rogers had a wry sense of humor, implying that *two* houses of government squabbling between one another would hasten our downfall. Maybe he provided some humorous exaggeration here, but this witticism reminds us that cooperation is better than conflict.

May 5
Greatness

The price of greatness is responsibility.

(Winston Churchill, stateman, prime minister of England during World War II)

Concise and expensive. Churchill led the British to persevere during World War II and never shirked his responsibility for the success or failure of the combat. If you expect to be great, the price is unwavering acceptance of responsibility for your own actions and omissions.

May 6
The Prize

There is nothing on this earth more to be prized than true friendship.

(St. Thomas Aquinas, philosopher, theologian and Saint Circa, 1225 AD)

We desire love and support. Beyond family and marriage, we search for the loyalty of deep and genuine friendships. It is a rare treasure to obtain and must be nourished by both persons to sustain. As Churchill said, there is a price for "greatness," and it is responsibility. St. Thomas rates true friendship as one of the greatest treasures in this life. Greatness is linked to self-responsibility and accountability.

May 7
Precision

Age quod Agis.

(Do what you are doing.) (old Latin proverb)

Caution: Multitasking might be fast but inaccurate. The Roman proverb reminds us to concentrate on what we are doing at work or in our relationships. Distraction leads to disruptions and, sometimes, disasters. Overlooking a single iceberg led to the terrible loss of 1,500 souls aboard the *Titanic*.

May 8
World Peace

What can you do to promote world peace? Go home and love your family.

(Mother Teresa, founder of the
Missionaries of Charity religious order)

World peace? Some have stated that the history of mankind is a history of wars, interrupted by brief periods of peace, a small wonder that we yearn for the dawn of world peace. Mother Teresa had a small prescription for each of us. The call to go home and love your family sounds simple and limited. But imagine that each one who practiced this love would come back to the world beyond family, recharged with love and kindness for others. Is it too much to expect? Well, we may question its efficacy, but why not try it out?

May 9
Stability

So much of what is best in us is bound up in our love of family that it remains the measure of our stability. That is because it measures our sense of loyalty.

(Haniel Long, poet, novelist, publisher)

To be loyal is to be steadfast. Steady and persevering love and devotion to family breed good character and the ability to become stable and helpful to them and others in our community. It is said that the family is the key building block of society, and from that environment, we are educated to be virtuous. Stay close to family members even when work may relocate us far away from them.

May 10
Family—the Essential Classroom

There is no doubt that is around the family and the home are all the greatest virtues, the most dominating virtues of humanity are created, strengthened, and maintained.

(Winston Churchill, prime minister statesman)

To echo the words of Haniel Long, Sir Winston Churchill affirms that family and home life can have a predominant influence on the formation of our humanity. Today, many dismiss the bond of marriage and downplay the importance of caring devotion to children that we bring into life. Isn't it true that we are a reflection of what we and our parents were doing or dismissing in our earliest years?

May 11
What Perdures?

> *When all the dust is settled, and all crowds are gone,*
> *the things that matter are faith, family, and friends.*

(Barbara Bush, wife, first lady of the USA)

Honors, titles, and medals fade. Faith in God, family, and friends remain untarnished, sustaining, perduring. When we are gone, those who knew us will be happy because of our relationships with them, not the objects or "reviews" which we acquired. After passing on, some possessions will be left to our heirs or charities, but the goodness we shared with all will long be remembered.

May 12
Attitude

Attitude is a choice. Happiness is a choice. Optimism is a choice. Kindness is a choice. Giving is a choice. Whatever choice you make makes you. Choose wisely.

(Roy T. Bennett, author of inspirational thoughts)

Free will? Yes, we awake with this gift each day and, sometimes, are so unaware of it that we feel asleep, oppressed, driven by our daily routines that almost forfeit the blessings of freedom to be our best. Plato said, "Be kind because everyone you meet is fighting a greater battle." That said, why not chose kindness, giving, optimism to lighten the other's burden and receive as we give?

May 13
Some Paradoxes

The good you do today will be forgotten tomorrow.
Do good anyway. Honesty and frankness make you
vulnerable. Be honest and frank anyway.

(Kent M. Keith, American
writer and sociologist)

What does last? Approval, praise, social status? Most are transient and matter little to most other people. The rewards you most enjoy are those which come from doing what you perceive are the right and beneficial choices. If others turn against you or malign you, what of it? Whatever good comes of your good choices will enlighten and elevate someone and lift your own spirits.

May 14
Lost and Found

God never takes away something from your life without replacing it with something better.

(Billy Graham, evangelist)

Faith in our Creator is like the North Star to sailors. He is constant and can always guide us in the right direction to bring us safely home. Without faith in God to guide us, we are like the blind traveling through a jungle at darkest nighttime. The soul, which is humble, recognizes his limitations and confusions. If we blame fortune or luck for some loss, it might be as Billy Graham said, something else is what God decided is the better replacement. Worth another look?

May 15
Reputation Redefined

Be more concerned with your character than your reputation because you're your character is what you really are while your reputation is merely what others think you are.

(John Wooden, outstanding coach and motivator)

Coach Wooden reminds us that to reach success, we have to develop strengths which contribute to our common good. On the road to success, think more of what we make of ourselves than others think of us. Shed the burden of vanity as you gain the strength through generosity.

May 16
Mistakes Are Experiments

A person who never made a mistake never tried any-thing new.

(Albert Einstein, physicist)

How often do we hesitate to embrace new challenges or tasks because we fear failure? Do we think that failure will cause shame or loss of reputation? Such social pressure can deprive us of accomplishments, which come through or after multiple failures. Thomas Edison tried over nine hundred materials to find success with the first light bulb. When others discouraged him, he reminded them that his nine hundred tries were actually successful eliminations of materials. He was determined to find the critical material. Nine hundred tries to get it right, and on the 901st, he *did*.

May 17
Kindness—Universal Language

Kindness is the language which the deaf can hear and the blind can see.

(Mark Twain, born Samuel Clemens,
river pilot and novelist)

Every day in our calendar is a short period of time measured by the rotation of our earth toward and away from the sun. Performing a kindness each day might put some "golden ink" on each page of that calendar.

May 18
Happy?

Most folks are as happy as they make up their minds to be.

(Abraham Lincoln, sixteenth president of the USA)

Travel, fine food, sumptuous house, and grounds? Do these things, which some have in abundance, really make you happy? News of the lives of the rich and famous do not tell us they were all happy. Perhaps President Lincoln was on to something when he told us that happiness is a matter of self-determination.

May 19
Self-Determination

Happiness depends upon ourselves.

(Aristotle, philosopher and teacher)

From over two thousand years ago, a Greek philosopher taught that we have more to gain by taking on responsibility and self-reliance than anything else.

May 20
Simple Is Better?

Simplicity is the ultimate sophistication.

(Leonardo da Vinci, artist and author)

Years ago, designers at a medical company were discussing ways to improve a product. One path offered a simple approach. One technician asked, "Is the simple design really better?" And the senior designer replied, "No, not better. Actually, simple is the *best* approach."

May 21
Perseverance

Patience and perseverance have a magical effect before which difficulties and obstacles vanish.

(John Quincy Adams, sixth president of the USA and diplomat)

Our Founding Fathers were without "a script" as they guided our young nation after winning the Revolutionary War. President Adams counseled patience and perseverance as the means to dispel obstacles to progress. If he and the early founders had lacked those qualities, we might have never emerged as a strong and stable nation.

May 22
Quantity and Quality

Not how long but how well you have lived is the main thing.

(Seneca, Roman poet and satirist)

Quantity without quality, or quality lacking quantity, marks a critical relationship in matters of production and the enjoyment of life. We certainly look forward to many good years of life, but it is our duty to make our years a time of good quality for our good and that of all the persons we touch in our lifetimes.

May 23
Settle or Build?

Don't settle for what life gives you, make life better and build something.

(Ashton Kutcher, American actor, entrepreneur)

What separates the mediocre from the extraordinary? Ashton presents a thought about the complacency or the restless desire to improve something. Whether you are comfortable or poor, your drive to better yourself will power your future success and contribution to the world.

May 24
Dreams to Reality

Never underestimate the power of dreams and the influence of the human spirit. The potential for greatness lives within each of us.

(Wilma Rudolph, Olympic champion sprinter, winner of multiple gold medals)

A genuine champion, Wilma overcame childhood polio and believed her mother who said that she would walk again. She dreamed of, and believed in, winning. She more than fulfilled her dreams, winning gold medals in multiple Olympic Games over many years. She later became a teacher and a beloved iconic leader in desegregating her hometown. Dream small or dream *big*? It is up to you.

May 25
Extraordinary

People do not decide to become extraordinary. They decide to accomplish extraordinary things.

(Edmund Hillary, mountaineer)

He along with Sherpa guide, Tenzing Norgay, were the first climbers to reach the top of Mount Everest.

Sir Edmund Hillary did more than climb the highest mountains, he founded hospitals and schools for the Sherpa peoples of the Himalayas while maintaining a sense of humility. Not ordinary things were in his heart but the extraordinary. (As another month winds down, what's your level of desire?)

May 26
Limits, Real and Imagined

> *Don't limit yourself. You can go as far as your mind lets you. What you believe, remember, you can achieve.*

> (Mary Kay Ash, entrepreneur and philanthropist, founder of Mary Kay Inc., an international multibillion-dollar company)

Mary rose above discrimination in the workplace, invented a novel way of rewarding her "consultants" who sold her beauty products and endowed charitable groups to help others. She had faith in the power of belief, even accentuating it with this short saying to back it up: "If you think you can, you can. If you think you can't, you're right." Timely tip: Eliminate that ugly word from our vocabulary—*can't.*

May 27
Discovery, a Joy

You were designed for accomplishment, engineered for success, and endowed with the seeds of greatness.

(Zig Ziglar, American author, speaker
and motivational expert)

Finding a treasure is a joy. The treasure of finding the one you love or the work we are most suited to do elevates us to new heights. Zig seemed to have found these and shared his discovery with many. Here he says that we are designed, engineered, and endowed for accomplishment, success, and the seeds of greatness. What a claim! But he is right. We obtain these treasures. We just have to find out how that works out in our lives. A hint: He also said, "You can get everything in life you want if you will just help enough other people get what *they* want."—sounds a lot like the Golden Rule and the scriptural advice to serve others.

May 28
Happy?

Success is not the key to happiness. Happiness is the key to success. If you love what you are doing, you will be successful.

(Albert Schweitzer, doctor, theologian, medical missionary)

Doctor Schweitzer reverenced life and service to humanity. Finding what we love to do may provide a career path, which induces happiness. By working diligently on that path, you will secure success.

May 29
Defined or Confined

Don't let others define you. Don't let the past confine you. Take charge of your life with confidence and determination, and then there are no limits on what you can do or be.

(Michael Josephson, attorney, professor, and founder of the Joseph and Edna Ethics Institute)

Counselor Josephson insists on honesty and founded an institute to cultivate ethical behavior in young people. Belief in working hard, taking responsibility, and being trustworthy are some of the principles that guide us to have rational self-confidence and determination. If you are acting right, you will be doing right.

May 30
Joy

> *All my life through, the new sights of nature made*
> *me rejoice like a child.*

(Marie Curie, physicist, chemist, and pioneer in radiation)

The Polish-born scientist, with her husband, Pierre, and their associate scientist, Henri Becquerel, earned a Nobel Prize in physics, was considered *the* pioneer of radioactivity. With all her intellectual capacity, she still found childlike joy in nature. Are we missing out on the gift of sunrises or mirrorlike lakes or autumn storms of color? Time to take another look at the outdoors?

May 31
Memorial Time

The soldier, above all other people, prays for peace, for he must suffer and bear the deepest wounds and scars of war.

(Douglas MacArthur, five-star general and commander of the Pacific Forces in World War II)

A general must shoulder the heavy burden of command and suffers when his troops are injured or killed in battle. But command he must. His insight about peace reveals that he and all who defend our country should be praying and working for peace to replace conflict.

June 1
Results

I am not a product of my circumstances. I am a product of my decisions.

(Stephen Covey, PhD, educa-
tor, author of *The 7 Habits of Highly
Effective People* and entrepreneur)

Dr. Covey shows everyone how to control what is in his *own* power to control. The good habits described in his book and augmented in his training materials help thousands improve their lives by taking command of their time and actions. Worth a look?

June 2
Inevitability

> *You can cut down all the flowers, but you can't stop*
> *spring from coming.*

(Pablo Neruda, Chilian poet and senator)

What is in our power, we can control. What is beyond our power is not. As Dr. Covey wrote, it is a waste of time and energy to fight events or powers beyond our control, so it is best to differentiate and tackle what *is* changeable.

June 3
Learning from Mistakes

A man must be big enough to admit mistakes, smart enough to profit from them, strong enough to correct them.

(John C. Maxwell, pastor, author, and founder of EQUIP, a nonprofit leadership training institute)

Mistakes are inevitable. Taking a look back a few days or years and we can isolate a few really startling examples. But did we admit, profit from, and perform course corrections from them? It's wise to look at our mistakes as notes in the book of our lives, which we have circled and singled out for profitable modifications of behavior.

June 4
Divine Assistance

> *I have held many things in my hands, and I have lost them all. But whatever I have placed in God's hand, that I still possess."*

(Martin Luther, priest, theologian,
Augustinian monk, and reformer)

Trusting in God, who surpasses all human limitations, was Martin Luther's best course. What we cannot do, God can! Finding our limitations and trusting in the Creator will provide unlimited resources for all the good we hope to do for all we meet in this lifetime.

June 5
Human Assistance

> *Relationships are based on four principles: respect,*
> *understanding, acceptance, and appreciation.*
>
> (Mahatma Gandhi, politi-
> cal leader and ethical teacher)

As social beings, we find comfort in our human relationships. What we want, the four principles which Gandhi identified, we have to offer to another *and* another until we have a genuine support group based on giving as well as receiving.

June 6
A Genuine Friend

There is no possession more valuable than a good and faithful friend.

(Socrates, Ancient Greek philosopher)

Many are called "friends" who might better be called acquaintances or neighbors. We may live or work close by others, but a "true friend" is rare because he or she will be kind, loyal, candid, and forgiving. As Mahatma Gandhi recalls, good relationships are founded on respect, understanding, acceptance, and appreciation. And we have to offer it in order to merit it in return.

When you ask God for a gift, be thankful if He send not diamonds, pearls or riches but the love of real true friends.

(Helen Steiner Rice, American writer of
religious and inspirational poetry)

Robinson Crusoe, hero of a novel, was the lone survivor of a shipwreck. Castaway on a Pacific island with all the treasures of the ship which he was able to salvage, he was deeply unhappy. Why? He had no companions at all. Ms. Rice identifies the real treasures in life as "real true friends." Wise woman.

June 7
Gratitude—Hard to Calculate

The hardest arithmetic to master is that which enables us to count our blessings.

(Eric Hoffer, American author and philosopher)

Anyone living in a free country, enjoying sufficient food, clothing, shelter, and some way of making a living, is essentially well blessed. Hoffer asks us to look at what we have and give it a thoughtful accounting. Most folks take note of what they do not have or zealously pursue but do not consider with gratitude that which they already enjoy. That is the calculation worth internalizing.

June 8
Grateful Coming and Going

Gratitude makes sense of our past, brings peace for today, and creates a vision for tomorrow.

(Melody Beattie, American
author and motivator)

Why are you happy today? Are you waking up with a sense of blessings that are behind you and still expecting more to arrive as you go about your day's work? Are you glad that you envision the future ahead with many opportunities to do more for your family and friends tomorrow and into the future times ahead? What came over you? Likely, it was that sense of gratitude for so much, and still more, to come!

June 9
Discussions

Great minds discuss ideas. Average minds discuss events. Small minds discuss people.

(Eleanor Roosevelt, first lady of the USA)

Every discussion finds topics and explores them. Is our curiosity focused on the higher levels of discovery or the mundane? Thinking is one of the foremost qualities of humans, and the ability to process thought and exchange concepts in speech is remarkable. Before each discussion, it may be profitable to focus on topics of greater relevance and elevate our discourse.

June 10
Sight and Vision

> *The only thing worse than being blind is having sight but no vision.*

(Helen Keller, author, activist, the
first person, while blind and deaf, to
attain a BA degree in fine arts)

Helen Keller led the way to overcome severe disabilities and illuminates two words. The *blind* person is deprived of sight, but the person without a *vision* is in a worse condition due to a lack of understanding or positive outlook. Are we persons of vision? Most of us see but do not have a vision.

June 11
Luck or Hard Work?

Some succeed because they are destined to, but most succeed because they are determined to.

(Henry van Dyke, American educator and clergyman)

How would you know that you are destined to succeed without signs of inborn talent or inherited genius? Without such clear signs of dominant talent, most of us must put our "shoulders to the wheel," plow ahead against the storms, and reach success by force of will and self-discipline.

June 18,
Growth

Commit to growing yourself. Stay present, and handle one situation at a time with an open mind and heart. Trust yourself and in the universe that everything will work out in the end.

(T. Harv Eker, author and motivational speaker)

What greater resource do you have than yourself? What else is more valuable to you than your own well-being and growth? Looking at challenges as opportunities for bettering yourself transforms and frees each of us for positive thoughts and actions. The universe is on your side? That may take faith, but why not look at it through the lens of enormous possibilities that exist out there for our particular successes which lie just ahead of us even in the darkest times.

June 13
Gifts

> *Talent is God-given. Be humble. Fame is man-given. Be grateful. Conceit is self-given. Be careful.*

(John Wooden, winning basketball coach)

Balancing the gifts which come our way is important. As the championship-winning coach, Wooden reminds us, distinguishing and evaluating our "gifts" guides our conscience to behave well, avoiding excessive pride.

June 14
Perspective

Yesterday I was clever, so I wanted to change the world. Today I am wise, so I am changing myself.

(Rumi, also known as Jalāl ad-Dīn Muhammad Rūmī, Persian poet and mystic)

The mystic Rumi sees what many do not perceive what is beyond our power, adding, "If you can't change your fate, change your attitude." Modern psychologists echo this by asking, "Why must everyone around you change to improve your life?" Doesn't it cost less effort to change and adapt oneself rather than demanding that "the world change" to suit you?

June 15
A Kind Act

Remember, there's no such thing as a small act of kindness. Every act creates a ripple with no logical end.

(Scott Adams, cartoonist and author)

Continuity of an action is amazing. Watch when a stone is dropped into a still pond. You can see the ripples extending outward toward the end of your visual field. Does the action stop there? We do not see the waves below the surface or the fish which might swim away from the disturbance or the fisherman on the far side of the pond who may now catch that redirected fish. Ah, supper! Scott Adams reminds us to monitor our actions, noting that even what may seem small, like a kind act, will keep on resonating in the world.

June 16
Timely Acts

You cannot do a kindness too soon, for you never know how soon it will be too late.

(Ralph Waldo Emerson, essayist, poet, philosopher)

Beyond the value of a kind act is the urgency of timeliness. When is a kind act best done? Since as the poet said that we never know the extent of our time here, the best time would be the present time. As he also said, "The purpose of life is not to be happy, it is to be useful, to be honorable, to be compassionate."

June 17
Longevity

Perhaps you will forget tomorrow the kind words you say today, but the recipient may cherish them over a lifetime.

(Dale Carnegie, writer and lecturer, well-known for many self-help books like *How to Win Friends and Influence People*)

As you look back on your own happiness, contentment, or achievement, is there a parent, teacher, coworker, or spouse who gifted you with some kind, encouraging words which fueled your rise to success? Why not repay them or others who are in need of similar acknowledgment?

June 18
Urgency

Life's most persistent and urgent question is, "What are you doing for others?

(Martin Luther King Jr., pastor, civil rights leader)

We look at the world through our own eyes, and we are constantly tuned into a "What's in it for me" outlook as we compete for survival and get ahead in this world of needs and wants. Pastor King reverses this perspective, asking us to focus on the biblical precept of serving others. Why should we look outward? In serving, we are freed from excessive self-love, and our service becomes "prayer in action."

June 19
Leadership

> *A true leader does not set out to be a leader but becomes one by the equality of his actions and the integrity of his intent.*
>
> (Douglas MacArthur, American five-
> star general and statesman)

Every worker who aspires to be a manager or an executive, as he or she progresses in their fields, might examine this test of General MacArthur. Are you desiring fame and fortune or determined to merit a role of higher responsibility by way of evenhanded treatment and ethical behavior toward all.

June 20
Productive Leaders

*Leaders don't create followers, they create more
leaders.*

(Tom Peters, American author of *In
Search of Excellence*, motivator)

When you hear that someone in the company has been promoted a rank or two, do you recall that the person above him or her
played a role in developing that person to take on more responsibility? So are you ready for a promotion? Are you outstanding in your
job and recognizable for promotion? Tom Peters asserted that one of
the little big things you must to do to succeed is become a "paragon
of personal responsibility." Be that, and they will find you.

June 21
Privilege

Leadership is a privilege to better the lives of others.
It is not an opportunity to satisfy personal greed.

(Mwai Kibaki, third president of Kenya, Africa)

A position of power? A position of responsibility? Any leadership role confers both power and a concomitant role of responsibility for the well-being of those who you will lead and the benefit of your company, group, or team. Often, leaders seek power foremost and underperform when it comes to accepting personal responsibility for his people and the success of their projects. The worst outcome is the abuse of power to satisfy personal greed. When your turn comes to lead, let it be for the common good and strive for optimum results.

June 22
Contributions

Every person has a longing to be significant, to make a contribution, to be a part of something noble and purposeful.

(John C. Maxwell, pastor and author)

Everyone who does a job well can empower his or her associates. He or she is a leader by example. And when you help others, with or without a leadership title, your work does make a contribution to the individuals with whom you interact and the group you work for. You build up your own confidence and are a part of something noble.

June 23
Improvement

There's only one corner of the universe you can be certain of improving, and that's yourself.

(Aldous Huxley, English writer and philosopher—his books include *Brave New World*)

If you, like many, want to make the world a better place, then the most significant starting point is within you. Look at what you have done and left undone to get a perspective on the remaining work of self-improvement still ahead, and start on that today!

June 24
Perspective

> *"What are you doing," asked the King while inspecting construction of a structure in his capital city. Three workmen replied, and the first said, "Making a living, carving and setting these stones." The second one said, "Laying these stones straight and strong to last for years." The third man replied, "I am building a cathedral for prayer and worship." Each did good and honest work. Who might have felt the best about his efforts? What perspective do you bring to and take home from your work?*

(Anonymous)

June 25
Before and After

> *Before you are a leader, success is all about growing yourself. When you become a leader, success is all about growing others.*

(Jack Welch, CEO of General Electric)

To take a leadership role, you either start a business or are promoted up the ranks of another company. Either way, you have to develop your talent until you are either recognized as specifically valuable to a company, or you take on the role of founder of your own enterprise. But once there, your key responsibility is generating future leaders within the business if there is to be a successful outcome.

June 26
Resistance and Tailwinds

> *When everything seems to be going against you,*
> *remember that the airplane takes off against the*
> *wind, not with it.*

(Henry Ford, founder of Ford Motor Company)

As you begin to make your contributions to the success of your enterprise, you will find headwinds and storms opposing you. As Henry Ford observes, an airplane must head *into* the winds to achieve *lift*, or there will be no flight. So the headwinds, in a sense, are an essential component of success. They fight you and also help to lift you to the next level of accomplishment.

June 27
Stand or Sit?

Courage is what it takes to stand up and speak.
Courage is also what it takes to sit down and listen.

(Winston Churchill, prime minister of England in WWII)

A Great Leader, Mr. Churchill faced opposition in his life and the perils of enduring the battles of WWII. But he knew well how to apportion speaking and listening so that he both took counsel, and then wisely commanded his officers to accomplish victory. His reward was being voted out of office after the war, but he returned to lead his country again because of his resilience.

June 28
Freedom to Speak

Whoever would overthrow the liberty of a nation must begin by subduing the freeness of speech.

(Benjamin Franklin, ambassador and statesman of the USA)

Freedom is essential to human happiness. Since freedom means many things to a variety of people, they must enjoy the freedom to exchange ideas on what they need and desire. If the freedom or freeness, as Franklin termed it, is constrained or eliminated, the hearts of men grow angry and rebellious. Freedom to express ideas and debate their values guarantee that each one feels they possess the oxygen of freedom and the opportunity to thrive.

June 29
Earning Freedom

Freedom is the greatest fruit of self-sufficiency.

(Epicurus, Greek philosopher who
espoused happiness through self-sufficiency and the company of good friends)

As we know, "freedom is not *free*" but has to be earned. The ancient Greek philosopher urged us to be accountable and live happily by self-reliance and the enjoyment of good friends' company. An apparently simple formula, but what it demands is the fulfillment of all that best within us—the development of our good character and embrace of our true friends. Quite a program after all?

June 30
The Battle Required of Us

Freedom is the sure possession of those who, alone, have the courage to defend it.

(Pericles, general, author, and statesman of Ancient Athens)

A "not my job" attitude affects us in big and small ways. Taking responsibility at work and home, school, and community means that we are always putting in the effort to make our lives secure, free, and ethical. Each and every child must learn that from parents' lives, teachers' lessons, and the sacrifice of our country's defenders.

July 1
Reactions

You can't change how people treat you or what they say about you. All you can do is change how you react to it.

(Nicky Gumbel, Anglican pastor and author)

Life is seldom fair due to our individuality and differing amounts of gifts and energies. Sometimes others will complain about us or defame us, but that is their action. And as Pastor Gumbel reminds us, it is our job to control and adjust our reactions in order to regain equanimity.

July 2
Choice Exists

No matter what the situation, remind yourself, "I have a choice."

(Deepak Chopra, author, advocate of alternative medicine)

When facing people or events which threaten our reputations, careers, or our total well-being, the answer is not panic or retreat. The answers lie in reflection, analysis, decision, and action. Freedom to choose one's course liberates you from fear and paralysis. Choose to walk the open road instead of slogging through the swamp.

July 3
Surrender Is Fatal

Our greatest weakness lies in giving up. The most certain way to succeed is always try just one more time.

(Thomas A. Edison, inventor and entrepreneur)

When we encounter a roadblock in life, we are tempted to give up. It may be in a small or large matter of work or school, but giving up will not be productive. The man who invented the light bulb and other tools of modern life did not give up. In his life, he considered failures as "positive eliminations" of faulty materials or designs. To illustrate, Edison said, "I have not failed. I've just found ten thousand ways that won't work."

July 4
Independence and You

Be very careful what you say to yourself because someone very important is listening—you!

(John Assaraf, author, neurological researcher)

As we know, what people say to us will matter in proportion to their credentials. And in reality, what we say to ourselves, positive or negative messages, may carry the ultimate weight in our perceptions of life and even who or what we are. To maintain an independence from false notions and debilitating messages, evaluate your "self-talk" because it molds your personality.

183

July 5
Pressure

> *The next time you feel slightly uncomfortable with the pressure in your life, remember, no pressure, no diamonds. Pressure is part of success.*

> (Eric Thomas, author, minister, and public speaker)

Comfort is one of key rewards we all seek in life. It is ranked by Abraham Maslow just above security. Many people stop at comfort in life's quest for fulfillment. Pressure seems to be directly opposed to comfort, but in our work and efforts to go further, it might be an essential part of the climb to success. Eric tells us to be consistent despite pressure. It is part of the climb to the top where we reach esteem, and then self-fulfillment.

July 6
Enjoyment

Don't wait for something outside of yourself to make you happy in the future. Think how really precious is the time you have to spend whether it's at work or with your family. Every minute should be enjoyed and savored.

(Earl Nightingale, author and
motivational speaker)

What might be missing in our search for happiness? Could it be Fame, Fortune, or renown? Maybe it is right in front of us, surrounding us, and still unappreciated. How much of our lives is right at hand, like family and work? Do we focus on what "they and it" really mean to us and how much we could enjoy family and the workplace, if we really "tune into them and it?"

July 7
Fears—a Positive Stress?

Just remember, you can do anything you set your mind to, but it takes action, perseverance, and facing your fears.

(Gillian Anderson, American actress)

Overcoming fear is essential to becoming a successful actress, surgeon, jet pilot, or any part of the armed forces. We may not eliminate fears, but learning to deal with them and accepting them as part of the human jungle we live in, take us to a level of courage to do what must be done to succeed.

July 8
Happiness = Smart Arithmetic

Happiness adds and multiplies as we divide it with others.

(Anonymous)

What a magic commodity! Happiness is a good thing, but selfish ownership of happiness is not wise. Why keep our happiness to ourselves when by sharing it, we can expand it continuously without losing it? Adding a kind word, a genuine compliment, offering assistance because you are happy and feeling generous will expand that spiritual state of bliss, not diminish it. Be happy, but don't hoard *it*!

July 9
Components

> *They say a person needs just three things to be truly happy in this world. Someone to love, something to do, and something to hope for.*

(Allan K. Chalmers, Scottish physician and author)

Dr. Chalmers lists components of happiness we must focus on. First is a devoted companion to love and who will return that love. Next, a career or purposeful work, and lastly, focusing on a future accomplishment. All three, and likely more, are out there in the complex everyday world in which we move. If we have already found all three, focus on them. If not, do not delay your search and discovery of these and any other goal to help you acquire happiness.

July 10
Attitude and Contentment

Happiness doesn't depend on what we have but how we feel toward what we have. We can be happy with little and miserable with much.

(William D. Hoard, governor of
Wisconsin and newspaper editor)

Truly happy or grumpy unhappy? Either description could fit the poor or the rich man, depending on how he evaluated the quality of his prosperity. A man with a small farm and loving family surpasses the happiness of a vastly rich man who is discontent with his wealth and family turmoil. Evaluate the quality of your life before saying I am unhappy.

July 11
Gratitude

Let us be grateful to people who make us happy.
They are the charming gardeners who make our
souls blossom.

(Marcel Proust, French novelist)

Proust searched for the meaning of life and self-identity. His poetic style compliments those who help us to become our best selves. In order for plants to blossom, there must be gardeners who plant and tend the plants or bushes until they can come into flower and full bloom as do our parents and teachers. To these, we owe our debts of gratitude.

July 12
Responsibility

No person will make you happy unless you decide to be happy. Your happiness will not come to you. It can only come from you.

(Ralph Marston, football player and author)

From early childhood onward, we received so much from our parents and extended family members. Likely, we perceived happiness derived from the gifts and the attention which they freely gave us. As we grew older and more independent, the world around us gave little and asked much. To mature, we have had to make our own way, find joy in work, and make good friends. As Mr. Marston says, "It is our responsibility to create our happiness."

July 13
Look in the Mirror (Carefully)

What you do today can improve all your tomorrows.

(Ralph Marston, author)

What is looking back at you from the mirror? It is your own image. Is it smiling, anxious, thoughtful, quizzical? That "you" there is a snapshot of the person who is beginning the process of making him or herself productive, nurturing, educating, healing, or something else of value to oneself and others. Mr. Marston puts the onus on each one to create his or her own value and happiness. And it begins with the actions of this day.

July 14
Gifts of Value

Everywhere you go, take a smile with you.

(Sasha Azevedo, actress, photographer, survivor)

Gifts bring joy but are not always expensive, found in stores, or heavy. As Ms. Azevedo points out, a smile can be inexpensive, portable, enjoyable, and renewable. A smile will trigger a relaxation or invitation or speak or simply respond with another warm smile. Despite carrying around with us our heavy "backpack of worries," we could offer a smile to others who seem burdened with worry or sorrows. Their "backpack" might be heavier than our own, and a smile will show understanding and compassion.

July 15
Your Thoughts—Quality or Not?

The happiness of your life depends upon the quality of your thoughts.

(Marcus Aurelius, Roman emperor and stoic)

An emperor who led Rome in a time of peace, Marcus Aurelius directs us to evaluate our thoughts and their quality. Thoughts which come and go, composed of trivialities and quarrels, might be just a gigantic waste of brainpower. Examine, rank, and eliminate the trivial or negative and leave room for kind, creative, productive thoughts to converse within your mind. As was said, "The thought is father to the action." And so let your thoughts be of the highest quality to produce good offspring.

July 16
Centered?

Until you are happy with who you are, you will never be happy with what you have!

(Zig Ziglar, salesman, author, and motivator)

In life, our many activities, many tasks, constantly moving, reacting to changing demands put stress on us and can upset or put us in an off-balanced emotional and mental state. Mr. Ziglar had ten rules for success, and one of them commanded, "Evaluate where you are." When we become conscious of who we are, we feel "centered" and in charge of our lives and future directions. Happy? Then your possessions, status, family, and career are likely in balance. Unhappy? Maybe it is time to reassess many aspects of our lives.

July 17
Get or Give

You cannot always have happiness, but you can always give happiness.

(Alyson Noël, American author)

During the darkest of time when happiness eludes us, we can still provide some comfort, guidance, sustenance to others who are needy. And even if these acts do not immediately reverse our discontent, we are performing a service which brings help, joy, and even some happiness to others. Will we always be on the receiving end of life's gifts? Likely not. But it will always be in our power to reach out to help others survive and thrive.

July 18
Goals

If you want to be happy, set a goal that commands your thoughts, liberates your energy, and inspires your hopes.

(Andrew Carnegie, American indus-
trialist and philanthropist)

Goal—an objective to reach, to accomplish, an effect which you believe is worth attaining for your benefit and the good of others. A saying warns, "Unless you have a destination planned out, any road will do." The traveler who starts out on land or sea without a home or port to find will likely never reach the desired place. Happiness is a universal desire, but as the successful Mr. Carnegie asserted, do more, choose a goal which channels the powers of your mind, energies, and hopes.

July 19
A Smile's Value

The value of a smile—it costs nothing but creates much. None are so rich they can get along without it, and none are so poor but are richer for its benefits.

(Dale Carnegie, author and motivator)

Mention a smile you received, and you will smile just by remembering that sign of greeting or approval. Recall a smile you gave and think of how it evoked a brightening of the eyes and elevated the mood of the receiver. Mr. Carnegie's thought about a smile concludes, "It creates happiness in the home, fosters goodwill in business, and is the countersign of friends." Quite an energy in a tiny package!

July 20
Consistency

Spread love everywhere you go. Let no one ever come to you without leaving happier.

(Mother Teresa, founder of a religious order and a saint)

A saint who embraced the poor and needy shared her life and energies in giving relief to others who were suffering. Her message of spreading good energy to all can go forward through focused concern for others. Charity is more than dollars which you donate; it exists in the care and respect you give to everyone you meet.

July 21
The Challenge of Change

Your life does not get better by chance. It gets better by change.

(Jim Rohn, American entrepreneur and author)

Psychologists say that most of us fear change almost all of the time! Unsettling events or attitudes of the persons closest to us which change disturb our mode of living or equanimity. But to make things better than they are, we must accept the process of change. Drop a bad habit, develop a good one. Take a course, repair a relationship, seek a better job, but do what must be done to create a better situation. It's a challenge but a bridge to a better life.

July 22
Ask and You Shall Receive—Biblical Wisdom

If you don't go after what you want, you'll never have it. If you don't ask, the answer is always no. If you don't step forward, you are always in the same place.

(Nora Roberts, American author)

Afraid of rejection? An unasked question always registers as a wasted opportunity in the world of decisions. Ms. Roberts recommends action, not retreat. What are we doing when we silence ourselves out of fear? Likely getting our just desserts, yes?

July 23
Big or Little

> *Keep away from people who try to belittle your ambitions. Small people always do that, but the really great make you feel that you, too, can become great.*

(Mark Twain, American author)

Mentors and trustworthy advisors—where are they? Looking for great teachers among the unlearned or failures in life is useless. As the saying goes, "I never asked a poor man for a job." That should tell the tale. Seek wisdom from the wise, success from the accomplished. The man who is ready to belittle your ambitions probably has a thin record of personal accomplishments.

July 24
Becoming

We know what we are but know not what we may become.

(William Shakespeare, English playwright)

Shakespeare tells us to look deeper and perhaps believe in the greater self which we may become. As we dream big dreams and create a plan to make them come to be, stay the course, avoiding the small-minded who have not achieved much but will obstruct our personal growth.

July 25
Unique Product

> *You weren't an accident, you were deliberately*
> *planned, specifically gifted, and lovingly positioned*
> *on the earth by the master craftsman.*

(Max Lucado, American author and pastor)

Christian faith strongly asserts that a loving God has designed and chosen each one of us in a unique way to perform a special function in time on this planet. Accordingly, we must get on with our lives, confident that the good that we do is timely and designed to fit a plan to benefit all that we meet and the lives we touch directly and even indirectly.

July 26
Miracles

You can hope for a miracle in life, or you can realize that your life is the miracle.

(Robert Breault, operatic tenor)

Everyone is a miracle of God's plan? In the course of striving to survive our own lifetimes, we seem to miss that point. We are so occupied by the work of growing up, learning, and earning in order to survive that we grow unconscious of the wonder of our own birth, development, and unique contributions to our world.

July 27
Improvement

There is only one corner of the universe you can be
certain of improving, and that is your own self.

(Aldous Huxley, philosopher and author)

While we dream of making the world a better place, the job is sufficiently large and complex. But if each of us is determined to follow Huxley's precept, then each would make a significant contribution to that goal. Research the construction of any very tall modern building and you would find that thousands of people of mental and physical skills teamed up to design, build, and furnish that gigantic office tower. So without a doubt, each one involved played a significant part in the final product.

July 28
Time—a Paradox

> *Time is free, but it's priceless. You can't own it, but you can use it. You can't keep it, but you can spend it. Once you've lost it, you can never get it back.*

> (Harvey Mackay, best-selling author and columnist)

Puzzling thoughts about something we all prize, use, misuse, lose, and repurpose as we grow wiser to make the world better in whatever role we play, we must respect the paradoxes listed by Mr. Mackay and get right to it. That is, "Do it, whatever that thing you mean to do, now. Today."

July 29
Good Math

*To solve the human equation, we need to add love,
subtract hate, multiply good, and divide between
truth and error.*

(Janet Coleman, British historian and professor of medieval political thought)

What an equation! It's a brilliant solution and guide to desirable moral behavior and worth posting on our bulletin boards.

July 30
Good Seeds—Prerequisites for a Good Harvest

Do not judge each day by the (future) harvest you reap but by the seeds that you plant.

(Robert Louis Stevenson, Scottish
author of fiction and poetry)

Look at today and what we are planting. The future harvests of crops such as, ideas, wealth, and success are generated by the actions of today. However long it takes to reach the harvest, regard the quality of what we plant today.

July 31
Playing Relates to Age

We don't stop playing because we grow old. We grow old because we stop playing.

(George Bernard Shaw, Irish playwright, critic, activist)

Humans love each other and their dogs and cats. We frequently watch our pets as they play and tussle, roll together, and finally sleep in a tangle of fur and upended paws. Maybe that play keeps them young and happy. Sometimes we humans forget to continue the enjoyment of playtimes we shared in days of our youth. Recapture the fun and elation of play even if it's just frisbee toss or at a board game. Winning and losing graciously is rejuvenating!

August 1
Park or Ride

The road to success is dotted with many tempting parking spaces.

(Will Rogers, actor, comedian, commentator)

Why stop when you're succeeding? What prevents you from going onward? When we cannot see the depth of the water or the height of the mountain, caution holds us back from a plunge or a climb. Still, on a road to success, don't take a detour or slip into an attractive parking spot. Keep on driving on!

August 2
Discouraging?

Tough times never last, but tough people do.

(Robert H. Schuller, pastor and televangelist)

What causes us to lose heart? The root of discouragement is the lack of heart or will to overcome disadvantages or roadblocks. Pastor Schuller believed, as do most successful people, that the impediments are temporary, just transient problems, but the winners are those who outlast these interruptions.

August 3
Astute or Perspicacious

Never argue with stupid people, they will drag you down to their level and beat you with experience.

(Mark Twain, American novelist and humorist)

If you want to dispute a point with someone, pick a learned adversary. Mark Twain cautions us to avoid wrestling in the mud with the "not-so-smart" or you will be deemed just as dull-witted as your opponent. Be astute or shrewd in conduct, conversation, and civility.

August 4
Opportunity

Opportunity is missed by most people because it is dressed in overalls and looks like work.

(Thomas A. Edison, American
inventor and entrepreneur)

Looking back in a family album, my dad, at age six, was dressed in overalls at work in his mom's grocery store in Alabama. He worked his way through school and took on drafting work at the start of the Electrical Age in New York City. Years later he finished up his career as an architect, designing part of the New York City subway system and large wastewater treatment plants in New York and New Jersey. He saw "opportunity in overalls" and made the most of his life by taking on those opportunities.

August 5
Freedom

America will never be destroyed from the outside. If we falter and lose our freedoms, it will be because we destroyed ourselves.

(Abraham Lincoln, president of
the USA and liberator)

Lincoln spoke of the greatest betrayal of our freedom which grants opportunities. Because we live in a land of freedom and almost unlimited paths to success, we must vigilantly guard it. On a personal scale, living up to our opportunities keeps us from faltering and destroying ourselves by shirking our responsibilities and our chances for self-advancement which leads ultimately to success.

August 6
Free Speech

Whoever would overthrow the liberty of a nation must begin by subduing the freeness of speech.

(Benjamin Franklin, inventor, scientist, and founding father of the USA)

Freedom of speech seems commonplace in ordinary times. We discuss our ideas with friends, neighbors, and coworkers, finding agreement or dueling with opposition in friendly fashion. But when one person or group takes an absolutist position, banning any contrary concepts, we feel imprisoned in the grip of a tyrannical iron fist.

August 7
Truth and Consequences

The further society drifts from the truth, the more they will hate those who speak it.

(George Orwell, English novelist, journalist, and critic)

In times of division and polarization, one group may grow to hate the ideas and the identities of those opposing them. If a truth is uncomfortable to one side, it may retaliate by hating or punishing the other. Stand by what is true because it is worth it, whatever the cost.

August 8
Discipline—Adversity

There will have to be rigid and iron discipline before we achieve anything great or enduring. Discipline is learnt in the school of adversity.

(Mahatma Gandhi, states-
man and spiritual leader)

The truly brave have in common, self-discipline and the endurance of adversity. To survive and thrive, one must control one's own person, body and soul. That degree of self-discipline comes from overcoming challenges from within and outside of ourselves. But it must be achieved in order to accomplish good and lasting results.

August 9
Belief

Believe that there is light at the end of the tunnel.
Believe that you might be that light for someone else.
Believe in each other. Believe the best is yet to come.
Believe in yourself. I believe in you.

(Kobi Yamada, author and entrepreneur)

Touch it, taste it, hold it, this "belief thing" seems hard to quantify, yet as we exercise belief in hope and progress and value and in ourselves, we are empowered. Who knows when you will be that only light at the end of a dark tunnel to transform someone you have yet to meet?

August 10
Rest—Essential to Life

We find rest in those we love, and we provide a resting place in ourselves for those who love us.

(St. Bernard of Clairvaux, Cistercian
monk and doctor of the church)

Life is action, movement, emotions we feel, thoughts which race through our minds. Sleep is filled with complex and fantastical scenarios. What balances these racing thoughts and dreams is rest. In love, we can find a peace which grounds us and which in turn grounds the ones we love. Not just emotion, love demands service and sacrifice. But the rewards are great.

August 11
Meaning

Love is just a word until someone comes along and gives it meaning.

(Paulo Coelho, lyricist, novelist)

A concept, a feeling, a dedication—what is love? The novelist who had a religious awakening says the one you come to love transforms the idea into a reality. If you have found your love, you may agree. If not, that transforming person may be just nearby. Be aware, and be receptive.

August 12
Generosity

> *Most people enter a relationship in order to get something. In reality, the only way a relationship will last is if you see your relationship as a place that you go to give and not a place that you go to take.*
>
> (Tony Robbins, author, coach, and philanthropist)

A balance of give and take, needs and wants demand their fulfillment. But in the most delicate arena of intimate relationships, marriage, and parenting, expecting to get more than to give is a recipe for unhappiness. Generosity first and reciprocity second is a good operating principle.

August 13
Aim Carefully

*Far too many people are looking for the right person
instead of trying to be the right person.*

(Gloria Steinem, American
writer, feminist, activist)

What we hope to have is not as important as what we should
hope to be.

August 14
Proportions

Remember that the best relationship is one in which your love for each other exceeds your need for each other.

(fourteenth Dalai Lama, born Lhamo
Thondup, Buddhist monk, spiritual leader)

In short, love beyond need, give beyond expectations of return. When he is asked, what is most important, The Dalai Lama often answers, "Have a good heart." And with that, he smiles as if knowing that you will fill in the rest.

August 15
Hide and Seek

The loveless never find love, only the loving find love, and they never have to seek for it.

(D. H. Lawrence, English novelist and poet)

What we seek is elusive unless we are prepared to find it. The poet urges us to be well prepared to find that person who is ready to give us love. We must first be a loving person or "that other" will always be hiding or hidden from us.

August 16
Finding Love

*It is not surprising that we keep looking for love.
All of us are nothing but vibrations of love. We are
sustained by love, and in the end, we merge back
into love.*

(Swami Muktananda, teacher of yoga,
meditation, and spirituality)

Born of love, nurtured by love of parents, seekers of love, givers of love and devotion—everyone is truly on a quest for a person to love and be loved in return. So the teacher has revealed a truth: We are going toward ultimate love in the time beyond this time. "Merge back into love" is a deep thought worth pondering.

August 17
Meaning—Purpose

The meaning of life is to find your gift. The purpose of life is to give it away.

(Pablo Picasso, painter, sculptor, ceramicist)

If you have found your gift and are proficient in it, then how do you give it away? The painter's insight urges working with abandon, and in that fury of proficient labor, your talent will reach many, as it were "given away."

August 18
Aim High

The greatest danger for most of us is not that our aim is too high and we miss it, but that it is too low and we reach it.

(Michelangelo, born Michelangelo di Lodovico Buonarroti Simoni, Italian artist, sculptor, architect, and poet)

Why not aim higher than what we think we can reach? False humility or true fear? One of the most famous, multitalented creative artists advised reaching above our limited estimations. What a legacy is his, one which has lasted for centuries.

August 19
To Serve

Service is the rent we pay for being. It is the very purpose of life and not something you do in your spare time.

(Marian Wright Edelman, founder of the Children's Defense Fund and advocate for disadvantaged Americans)

Our being here is sometimes taken for granted. We did not order up our existence, but it was given. Ms. Edelman reminds us that there is an obligation to pay for our stay in this "earthly hotel," and perform work which is beneficial to others. One thing she recommends is the role of education, either as a parent or a teacher or mentor. It is essential for "improving the lives of others and leaving your community and world better than you found it." To that goal, we are all called to be educators.

August 20
Your "Gift"

> *Everyone has a purpose in life, a unique gift of spe-*
> *cial talent to give to others. And when we blend this*
> *unique talent with service to others, we experience*
> *the ecstasy and exultation of our own spirit, which*
> *is the ultimate goal of all goals.*

> (Deepak Chopra, Indian American
> author and motivator)

Quite a claim! Doctor Chopra counsels us to discover our special gift and integrate that into service. To do this successfully brings on the highest levels of fulfillment. It may take effort to find and blend it into our careers, but it promises to serve others well and highly reward the diligent worker.

August 21
Challenges

Find a purpose in life so big it will challenge every capacity to be at your best.

(David O. McKay, American religious leader and educator, ninth president of the Mormon Church)

Who doesn't tend to shy away from challenges? But what happens when we meet and overcome them? A sense of accomplishment, relief, and growing sense of self-belief take over. To find a purpose which challenges every talent and strength, we possess seems extremely daunting. Ironically, it makes us the best we can be. As the author also said, "The privilege to work is a gift, the power to work is a blessing, the love of work is success!"

August 22
Value

> *Know your value. Confidence breeds success. Act like the person you want to become, and people will start seeing you as that person.*

(Mark M. Ford, author, entrepreneur, publisher)

Do you have faith in yourself? Did it come from sports, warm family relationships, and others' support? If faith in yourself is low or lacking, it might be time to take Mr. Ford seriously. Act strong, walk upright, and take on challenges with an air of assurance. Positive action evokes positive reactions.

August 23
Optimism

Optimism is the faith that leads to achievement.
Nothing can be done without hope and confidence.

(Helen Keller, author, activist, and lecturer)

Confidence—that faith in oneself springs from an attitude of optimism. Some deride the optimist, relegating him or her to "dreamer or fool." But expecting the best outcome is the road to improvement. Settle for this or strive for that. It is wiser to desire and strive for the best. Michelangelo warned that we aim low and then settle for that instead of attaining grand accomplishments.

August 24
Defined or Refined?

> *Don't let others define you, don't let the past confine*
> *you. Take charge of your life with confidence and*
> *determination, and there are no limits on what you*
> *can do or be.*

(Michael Josephson, attorney, lecturer, and philanthropist)

Defy artificial limitations. When we are taking control of our lives with confidence, the limiting thoughts of what was or whose opinions diminish us drift away. Take control, aim high, go forward.

August 25
Effective Action

Some people want it to happen, some wish it would happen, others make it happen.

(Michael Jordan, star basketball player, entrepreneur)

One of the people who "made it happen," Mr. Jordan is ranked among the top stars of professional basketball and now owns a professional basketball team. His attitude of "never say never" avoided self-limitation.

Our belief should be that fears are just illusions standing in the way of our success.

August 26
What and How

Experience tells what to do, confidence allows you to do it.

(Stan Smith, number one ranked tennis player)

If we learn what not to do by disappointments and what *to* do by better experiences, then the motivator, the catalyst for success, will be a confident attitude behind our future well-directed efforts.

August 27
Criticism, Good and Bad Kinds

Don't be distracted by criticism. Remember, the only taste of success some people have is when they take a bite out of you.

(Zig Ziglar, author, motivator, and entrepreneur)

Good criticism is what helps make your path smoother and upward. The negative, jealous criticism is not worth your attention.

August 28
Gifts to Exploit

Life is not easy for any of us. We must have confidence in ourselves. We must believe we are gifted for something and that this thing must be attained.

(Marie Curie, physicist, chemist, the
unique winner of two Nobel Prizes
in two different fields of science)

If we are God's unique creations, then Dr. Curie's assertion holds true. We are each gifted, and it is our responsibility to develop and exploit our gifts for the good of all.

August 29
Believe

Believe in yourself! Have faith in your abilities! Without a humble but reasonable confidence in your own powers, you cannot be successful or happy.

(Norman Vincent Peale, minister and author of *The Power of Positive Thinking*)

You did it! You have succeeded in various projects, made friends, started a family, and feel there is much more ahead of you. This should ground you in both areas, confidence in your power, and humility that there are enormous amounts of accomplishments ahead of you. Believe in those, and you are on the way.

August 30
Conquest

It is not the mountain we conquer but ourselves.

(Sir Edmund Hillary, mountaineer and first
man along with Tenzing Norgay, his Sherpa
Guide, to reach the summit of Mt. Everest)

Jobs, anxieties, shyness, lack of educational accomplishment, or a mountain? What do we feel prevents us from winning our victories? The eminent mountaineer, Sir Edmund, declares that "self-conquest" is primary. Whatever it will take, whether it's knowledge, will power, finding the right guides, help is actually abundant and not far away. We must seek, ask, and find.

August 31
Fears

> *Successful people have fears, doubts, and worries.*
> *They just don't let these feelings stop them.*

(T. Harv Eker, author, businessman and motivational speaker)

Success doesn't fall into our laps because we are sad or happy. Success can be blocked by fears and self-doubt. But a feeling is just an emotion to be managed and used to help, not hinder our life's progress. Positive attitude proves to bring positive results. As was said, "Don't race with your shoelaces untied."

September 1
Responsibility

If you take responsibility for yourself, you will develop a hunger to accomplish your dreams.

(Les Brown, American congress-man, TV and radio personality)

How often we wish good fortune will happen to us. Rather than depend upon some outside events, accept responsibility and take charge of our own efforts. It will fuel our sense of progress, and we will acquire that hunger to make our dreams a reality.

September 2
Hard Work

Keep your dreams alive. To achieve anything requires faith, belief, hard work, determination and dedication.

(Gail Devers, three-time Olympic gold medalist)

Competing at the Olympic level requires the best of everything you've got. And if your job is challenging, think of how many times the Gold medalist has trained, sacrificed, reimagined the victory ahead, and then willingly accepted the pain and boredom which made him or her the champion.

September 3
Dreams

> *Dreams are like stars. You may never touch them,
> but if you follow them, they will lead you to your
> destiny.*

(Liam James, Canadian actor)

Dreams, as goals, are more than fantasy. But to make the most of our dreams, we must believe in and work for their actualization and not give up. The North Star guides travelers because it is constantly in place. So too must our dream remain consistent and in view.

September 4
Desire

> *Focus more on your desire than on your doubt, and*
> *the dream will take care of itself.*

(Mark Twain, author and river pilot)

Life is likely unfair. While life is full of opportunities, it is hampered by doubts. If you doubt, you can reach your desire or doubt that there will ever be someone to help you along, you may fail to reach your goals. Keep your desire intense and bright. It will brush aside the troubling doubts.

September 5
Imagination

Logic will get you from A to B. Imagination will take you everywhere.

(Albert Einstein, physicist, Nobel Prize winner)

Charts and road maps show destinations, a schematic of places and distances to guide the traveler. To transform travel or other progressions in life, use your creative imagination. Some inventions in modern times became available due to a creative reshaping of a problem into a solution. If you can tap the power of your creative imagination, something, which troubles you today, may put you on the road to a fortune by next year.

September 6
Persistence

> *Dreams can come true, but there's a secret. They're realized through the magic of persistence, determination, commitment, passion, practice, focus, and hard work.*

> (Elbert Hubbard, American writer,
> artist, and philosopher)

Magic! Sounds wonderful—a rapid, painless process to make my dreams come true! Oh, yes, but there are some essential components such as listed by Mr. Hubbard. The seven components are challenging and comprise the price of success. Are you ready to pay the price?

September 7
Time

Never give up on a dream just because of the time it will take to accomplish it. The time will pass anyway.

(Earl Nightingale, radio personality
and author of motivational essays)

It takes too much time! A complaint offered by many who seek prompt gratification. Earl Nightingale had many insights on time and effort which when applied productively pay rich dividends. It takes time to compound your invested money. Building on itself over long periods can not just add to but also multiply those savings. To bring a product from concept through patenting to production and into the hands of customers, you must expend effort and time. Time? Use it or lose it!

September 8
Start

> *You don't have to be great to start, but you have to start, to be great.*

> (Zig Ziglar, author, top salesman, and
> renowned motivational speaker)

Among Zig Ziglar's ten rules for success is "Do it now." Zig urges us to plan and follow through to reach our goals but reminds us that no plan is successful without a start and a follow-through. Do you have a plan for success? Did you start on it as yet? Great!

September 9
Starting Points

Your present circumstances don't determine where
you can go. They merely determine where you start.

(Nido R. Qubein, CEO, president of
Highpoint University, motivational speaker)

Note the flexibility of your "starting point." It is not determinative of your life but is a platform you are standing on at the present time. With all you have learned and earned, you must begin again to lean into the future. Going for what you want means stepping forward with enthusiasm regardless of any present limitations you may have. Dr. Qubein came to America with just a few dollars and now heads a top university, serves on the boards of Fortune 500 companies, and also teaches both freshman and senior classes, pointing them toward success.

September 10
Change

> *You can't go back and change the beginning, but you can start and change the ending.*

> (C. S. Lewis, British writer and theologian, author of *The Narnia Chronicles*)

Echoing Dr. Quebein, theologian C. S. Lewis reminds us that no matter where we started from, we can control our own destiny and our destination in life.

September 11
Respect

One of the most sincere forms of respect is actually listening to what another has to say.

(Bryant H. McGill, author, activist, social entrepreneur)

Paying attention to what another says can be trying. Are we not most often "tuned into" ourselves, which causes both a loss of perception and disrespect to our companions? It was once asked, "What shows class?" The group agreed: "Showing respect to others and making them feel important." As Mr. McGill asserts, an active, receptive listening experience will show respect during a conversation. So how *do* we listen?

September 12
Legacy

> *The things you do for yourself are gone when you are gone, but the things you do for others remain as your legacy.*

(Kalu Ndukwe Kalu, Nigerian born
American political scientist)

From morning to nighttime, we labor at home or at work to pay the bills and sustain our families. We work also to find some measure of self-fulfillment. All that we do for ourselves is sustaining and gratifying. And as Mr. Kalu reminds us, a lifetime's work can be gratifying, benevolent, and lasting if it also benefits others.

September 13
Thoughts to Actions

> *Genius begins great works. Labor alone finishes them.*

(Joseph Joubert, French essayist and moralist)

A saying goes, "The wish is father to the thought," and from thought onward, we go to complete a work of genius. Creating music, art, a unique person? What really brings the genius to life? As with nature, it takes the maternal gift of gestation and labor to bring forth the unique product. You may "think up" a great project, but your labor is the critical element that brings it to full birth.

September 14
Security

If money is your hope for independence, you will never have it. The only real security in this world is a reserve of knowledge, experience, and ability.

(Henry Ford, American industri-
alist and business magnate)

Security is our first basic need. Food, shelter, rest, human company provide our foundation. But is money the whole answer? Mr. Ford points to other facets of life as the genuine keys to security. Without a plentiful supply of knowledge and understanding from our experiences, we can "lose our money." Abilities, which we acquire from work and apprenticeships, provide us with flexibility in choosing new work when we are displaced due to commercial disruptions.

September 15
Bravery

> *Bravery is the capacity to perform properly even when scared to death.*

(Omar N. Bradley, five-star US general
and first head of the joint chiefs of staff)

A war hero and respected leader of our troops, General Bradley cautions us that we cannot avoid fear but must manage it on all occasions. "When the going gets tough, the tough get going" might have also been a motto of his. His intelligent leadership and concern for his many troops proved him worthy of his definition of bravery. In all our conflicts, remember to perform properly.

September 16
Essential Actions

Never worry about the numbers. Help one person at a time, and always start with the person nearest you.

(Mother Teresa, saint and founder
of the Missionaries of Charity)

In a modern world consumed with calculating value by larger numbers, Mother Teresa counsels us to start small or rather locally with one person close by. Who do you know who might need your help or attention today? As Mother Teresa said, "Let us always meet each other with a smile, for the smile is the beginning of love." Can you smile and make some time for him or her today?

September 17
Good Thoughts

If you have thoughts, they will shine out of your faced like sunbeams, and you will always look lovely.

(Roald Dahl, WWII fighter pilot, inventor, and successful author of children's books)

Good thoughts create a happy attitude which generate a lovely welcoming smile. If love starts with a genuine smile and molds a face into softer, more caring expression. This opens the door to acceptance and friendship. Can you "evict" some negative thoughts today?

September 18
Letting Go

> *The more anger toward the past you carry in your heart, the less capable you are of loving in the present.*

(Barbara De Angelis, author on personal relationships, coach, and TV personality)

Letting go of anger removes a burden and makes room for loving thoughts and actions. Ms. De Angelis urges "evicting" anger which not only crowds our minds but acts like acid or poison would if swallowed and reached our guts. A semicomical and largely serious comment goes like this: "Holding onto anger is like taking poison and expecting your enemy to die." What form of "poison" should you purge from your heart today?

September 19
A Key to Exceptional Marriage

When I have learned to love God better than my earthly dearest, I shall love my earthly dearest better that I do now.

(C. S. Lewis, writer, theologian, and university professor)

A paradoxical statement about our relationships—when we accept God as our Creator and ultimate destiny, we begin to place Him above all others. And still, says Dr. Lewis, we then become capable of bestowing a love on our dearest earthly companion which is superior to that previous love. Why? In the right order come God, family, friends, and country. Are my priorities in order?

September 20
Challenges to Love

> *A man is lucky if he is the first love of a woman. A*
> *Woman is lucky is she is the last love of a man.*

> (Charles Dickens, English novelist
> and social critic—his works include *A*
> *Christmas Carol* and *Great Expectations*)

Luck? Good luck has been renamed hard work, meeting up with opportunity. If we hope to have luck in our closest relationships, we better be prepared with hard work on ourselves. As C. S. Lewis said, "The right priorities are critical. A person who puts God first, himself last, and his family first after God will be on the right road to becoming a loving and easily loved person." What should we do today to get on and stay on that path?

September 21
Reciprocity

Life is very simple. What I give out comes back to me. Today I choose to give love.

(Louise Hay, novelist and motivational author)

Actually, when we give out love, it may come back as a trickle or a great wave. Usually, our donations are returned in reduced measure, and that can discourage us. But when our giving brings back great returns, we feel blessed, and our store of generosity is replenished. If we give and give that which is good, the benefits to others, and lastly to ourselves, will be enough. "Give and it shall be given to you" (a good measure). As is written in the gospel of Luke, chapter 6, verse 38.

September 22
Magic Key

Love is the master key that opens the gates of happiness.

(Oliver Wendell Holmes Sr., American
physician, poet, and polymath)

Love—the composite of magnetic attraction, mutual delight, undivided devotion, and faithful service over all time is indeed a master key. Magic? In a sense, it seems like magic, a spell, a horrendous power. But actually, it is a growing up, a fulfillment of what God intended us to be. It is reaching for our ultimate "best self" in concert with another person under God's laws and tender providence. Looking for happiness? Try to obtain the key which Dr. Holmes says fits the gate. He is correct. See for yourself.

September 23
Words Are More than Sounds

Words do two major things. They provide food for the mind and create light for understanding and awareness.

(Jim Rohn, author, motivational speaker, and entrepreneur)

Many words preceded this quotation, and here we have a reflection on words. Mr. Rohn puts words under the microscope to remind us that they nourish us with information. But we must find the light of "cognizance" to deepen our understanding and internalize such sounds as love, service, devotion, dedication. This takes work, and discipline is essential. As he also said, "Discipline is the bridge between goals and accomplishment." Are we up to that challenge?

September 24
Banish Worries

No one can pray and worry at the same time.

(Max Lucado, author and pastor)

Worries about real problems which confront us: There are bills to pay, health to be regained or improved, and younger family members striving to become educated and self-sufficient. But a real trust in God, and addressing our cares to His providence, can alleviate our worries. As he quotes Philippians 4:6–7, "Do not be anxious about anything, but in every situation, by prayer and petition with thanksgiving, present your requests to God. And the peace of God, which transcends all understanding, will guard your hearts and minds in Christ Jesus."

September 25
Freedom

Resolve to be a master of change rather than a victim of change.

(Brian Tracy, Canadian American
author and motivational speaker)

Change is all around us and pushing us to adapt to the newer order of technology and business. Mr. Tracy urges us to master these "waves of change" rather than be pulled under and suffer or perish. We hold the power to be masters of our destinies, not victims of circumstances. How do I start on this course? Pick one essential task and do it. Begin.

September 26
Times—Good and Bad

> *Bad times, hard times, this is what people keep saying. But let us live well, and times shall be good. We are the times, such as we are, such are the times.*

> (St. Augustine, theologian, philosopher, and bishop)

In light of this saying, we make the weeks and years of our lives to be days of quality or dissatisfaction. St. Augustine puts it briefly, "God provides the wind, man must raise the sail."

September 27
Vessels of Light

> *The more light which you allow within you, the brighter the world you live in will be.*

> (Shakti Gawain, New Age personal development author)

Poetic reminder of the Gospel saying, "Let your light so shine before men that they may see your good works and glorify your Father which is in heaven" (Matthew 5:16).

September 28
The Right Order of Things

> *They try to have more things or more money in order to do more of what they want so they will be happier. The way it actually happens is the reverse. You must be who you really are, then do what you need to do in order to have what you want.*

(Shakti Gawain, author)

Everyone is unique and has unique gifts to share. If you find your gift and exercise it, then you will find true fulfillment. Who are you in reality? What special gifts do you have? Have you utilized them? Go ahead and see what happens!

September 29
Giving

It is possible to give away and become richer! It is also possible to hold on too tightly and lose everything. Yes, the liberal man shall become rich! By endowing others, he endows himself. (Proverbs 11: 24)

Advice given thousands of years ago can help us give when we fear that donating to the poor will deprive us of security. As the Scripture tells us, in giving to the needy, we will receive much over time in proportion to our generosity. "To help the poor is to honor God" (Proverbs 14:31).

September 30
Behavior

A soft answer turns away wrath, but harsh words cause quarrels. (Proverbs 15:1)

When attacked, we react. It is almost an automatic reflexive response to counterattack when someone is angry and demeaning to us. The Scripture cautions against replying angrily because that may only escalate the conflict. A better behavior may show the way to reconciliation and understanding. We can be better than an aggressor and win them over.

October 1
Tactics

Sometimes we need to lose small battles in order to win the war.

(Sun Tzu, Ancient Chinese general, strategist, and philosopher)

Giving back a mild answer or yielding a point in an argument is wiser than wasting effort on retaliation when it allows room for future agreement and a greater victory later on.

October 2
Tactics

Appear weak when you are strong and strong when you are weak.

(Sun Tzu, Chinese general, strategist)

The general knew how to retreat and how to advance. As we encounter resistance in relationships or business, take notice of how well his tactics will assist you. Showing compliance psychologically unbalances the attacker, but showing strength compels him to back down.

October 3
Tactics

The greatest victory is that which requires no battle.

(Sun Tzu, Chinese strategist and philosopher)

Finally, the desired outcome of any angry engagement is a resolution without fighting and wounding the other party. In disputes and conflicts among a family or business associates, we are always better off when we arrive at a win-win settlement of our differences. Preserve what you must have and let the other have his share of victory, and you will continue on as friends, not enemies.

October 4
Follow Through

He who strongly desires to rise up will think of a way
to build a ladder.

(Anonymous Japanese proverb)

Paralleling an American proverb, "Where there is a will, there is a way," we cannot stop at thinking and wishing about reaching a goal. To get up, fashion a ladder. To go over a river, build a bridge. To win over an opponent, use the tactics of Sun Tzu.

October 5
Symbiosis

There has never been a great individual who did not have ordinary people at their side.

(Anonymous Japanese proverb)

No one does great things alone or in isolation. The surgeon, the teacher, the mother, the statesman, all have their assisting "team members" beside them, behind them, or in collaboration in some form of a network. Respect the talents and ideas of all your collaborators who play a significant part in your campaign for succeeding in any enterprise.

October 6
Experiences

You can either feel sorry for yourself or treat what has happened to you as a gift. Everything is either an opportunity to grow or an obstacle to keep you from growing. You get to choose.

(Wayne Dyer, self-help motivational speaker
and author of best seller *Your Erroneous Zones*)

Mr. Dyer puts it to us straight up. Choose to interpret your experience as an obstacle, and it becomes one. You stop moving ahead or interpret it as an opportunity, and you have found an instrument of self-improvement and growth. What will you do?

October 7
Present Tense—Today!

Your big opportunity may be right where you are now.

(Napoleon Hill, American self-help author
of a best seller book *Think and Grow Rich*)

Echoes of Dr. Dyer? What if where you work, you are researching, or making a home is the prime opportunity of your life? Is it not important to look over the many ways you can transform what seems to the ordinary to something extraordinary? How many inventions were born out of frustrations, or cures were found after baffling failures to cure illness? The men and women of yesterday have handed us the miracles of today because they did accept their moment in the present as a prime opportunity to make things far better.

October 8
Kindness

Wherever there is a human being, there is an opportunity for kindness.

(Seneca the Younger, Roman stoic philosopher, statesman, and dramatist)

Your mission is not necessarily in far off places. The philosopher reminds us that every day, close at hand are people we meet, work with, or are remotely connected to. Is anyone needy of some encouragement, understanding, or just a kind word of appreciation? The cost is little. The effect can be huge.

October 9
Add or Multiply?

Opportunities are multiplied as they are seized.

(Sun Tzu, general, strategist, and philosopher)

A general wants to make the most of any opportunity to advance or win. Sun Tzu urges us to realize the compounding effect of seizing an opportunity and making the most of it. In war, in peace, business, or family development, each opportunity we grasp will offer others to us. Opportunities are gifts. Why settle then for addition when multiplication of gifts is available?

October 10
Perception

> *When you rise in the morning, think of what a precious privilege it is to be alive, to breathe, to think to enjoy, to love.*

(Marcus Aurelius, Roman
emperor, stoic philosopher)

Do we have an attitude of gratefulness from the basic experience of awaking alive each day? The stoic thinkers embraced the world, endured much with patience, and carved happiness out of whatever was dealt to them. Wealth does not equal happiness, but happiness brings a kind of wealth. Each day's awakening offers us such choices as Marcus Aurelius wrote about two millennia ago.

October 11
Strength

Start by doing what's necessary, then do what's possible, and suddenly you are doing the impossible.

(St. Francis of Assisi, friar, deacon, mystic)

A humble monk who loved God and was a man of deep prayer and devotion to God tells us that we can perform exceptional things. His formula seems simple but wise. Start small, build, and you can finally execute gigantic accomplishments.

October 12
Willpower

Strength does not come from physical capacity. It comes from an indomitable will.

(Mahatma Gandhi, political ethicist
and reformer by nonviolent means)

By means of determination and perseverance, Gandhi over-turned colonial rule in India. He was a frail thin man in size, but his willpower made him a giant of social change. How strong is your willpower today? Maybe it needs a program of strenuous "exercise."

October 13
Size

The size of your success is measured by the strength of your desire, the size of your dream, and how you handle disappointment along the way.

(Robert Kiyosaki, American businessman, author, and entrepreneur)

Taking a look at his family and comparing it to a friend's family, Mr. Kiyosaki found that his own father, who was an educator, was well-off financially but not as successful as his friend's father who owned a business. He noted that the risk-taker gained more from his trials than his own father who has less to worry about. What do you desire to accomplish, dream of having, and are resilient to? These qualities contribute to the measure of your future success.

October 14
Stress and Toughness

*Good timber does not grow with ease. The stronger
the wind, the stronger the trees.*

(J. Willard Marriott, American entrepreneur
and founder of the Marriott Hotel Corporation)

Stress is ingrained in almost all our experiences. Perhaps they are present as Mr. Marriott indicates for the purpose of building our strength and resilience. His work built an empire and brought many men and women up to positions of responsibility and self-assurance. (Marriott's core values: Put people first, pursue excellence, embrace change, act with integrity, and serve our world.) He demanded excellence from his employees, and they gained from it.

October 15
Strong and Wise

As our heart summons our strength, our wisdom must direct it.

(Dwight D. Eisenhower, five-star general and president of the USA)

General Eisenhower commanded the combined armed forces which invaded and liberated Europe in World War II. He was strong but wise in orchestrating the talents of other top generals and directing the courageous landing of all army, navy, and air force warriors under his command. Without humility and wisdom, the results of that great effort might have stumbled or failed. Be strong and wise. The combination is essential.

October 16
Kindness

Tenderness and kindness are not signs of weakness and despair but manifestations of strength and resolution.

(Kahlil Gibran, Lebanese American poet and artist, author of a well-known book, *The Prophet*)

Emotional reactions such as kindness take us to a place of generosity, freeing us from self-centered concerns. The poet celebrates the one who can have empathy for others and bestow some words or actions out of compassion and strength. Do we bypass opportunities to give a hand up or an affirmation when it would do so much to help another human being?

October 17
Push-Ups and Pull-Ups

There are two ways of exerting one's strength. One is pushing down, and the other is pulling up.

(Booker T. Washington, American educator, author, orator, advisor to presidents, leader of the African American community in his time)

Strength is good, but the direction of strength determines its full worth. Are we out to get and reluctant to give? Mr. Washington presents a simple dichotomy: Are we lifting others up or trying to keep them down? One makes you a small person, the other a champion helping others to gain their own trophies in life.

October 18
Words and Actions

> *As we express our gratitude, we must never forget*
> *that the highest appreciation is not to utter words*
> *but to live by them.*

(John F. Kennedy, thirty-fifth
president of the USA)

Words arranged well can express our grateful thoughts. Beyond words, spoken or written, the president reminds us to live out our good thoughts as proof positive of our sentiments. The old adage "Actions speak louder than words" is not out-of-date at all.

October 19
Conscience

Self-respect and a clear conscience are powerful components of integrity and are the basis for enriching your relationships with others.

(Denis Waitley, American Naval Academy
graduate and motivational speaker)

In relating to our family, trust, love, service, and complete loyalty must be complete. Relating to business associates and our customers, similar amounts of care and fair dealings are requisites. Good conscience? It has great rewards. One is happiness.

October 20
Happiness

Happiness is the spiritual experience of living every minute with love, grace, and gratitude.

(Denis Waitley, Navy veteran
and motivational speaker)

Happiness? Are we happy? Does that mean the absence of pain or enjoyment of comfort or possessing wealth? Better: "Happiness" comes from a state of consistent fairness to ourselves and others. Clear conscience and self-acceptance lead to gratitude and peace.

October 21
Faith

Keeping busy and making optimism a way of life can restore faith in yourself.

(Lucille Ball, American actress, comedian, and TV producer)

Millions of viewers must have seen and enjoyed the vivacity and humorous performances of the plucky lady called Lucy! As she asserts, optimism as a dominant force in your daily life can restore self-confidence. Viewing her work, you might wonder, "Did she ever lack it?" Do you lack it? Try her formula because it certainly worked wonders for her!

October 22
Beliefs

> *Almost every successful person begins with two beliefs, the future can be better than the present, and I have the power to make it so.*

> (David Brooks, Canadian born
> American journalist)

Faith in oneself and faith in principles guide us along life's road. They point the way and post detour signs where appropriate. Neglect of key signposts can get us lost.

October 23
Faith and Courage

A man of courage is also full of faith.

(Marcus Tullius Cicero, consul of Rome, statesman and orator who defended the republic)

Cicero had faith, a belief in himself and in his country, which enabled him to bravely oppose the enemies of Rome. To be a statesman, a patriot, and to defy powerful enemies takes courage which is born in faith.

October 24
Faith and Hope

Most of the important things in the world have been accomplished by people who have kept on trying when there seemed to be no hope at all.

(Dale Carnegie, American writer and lecturer, father of the self-improvement movement)

For centuries, travel on horseback or horse-drawn carriages were the mainstays of transportation on land. Ships sailed only with the help of the wind or the power of oarsmen. Was there no hope for a machine? Someone must have stepped up and, by hope in the future and faith in applied mechanics, developed a steam engine, followed by the late nineteenth-century combustion engines which gave us autos and jets. What are you dreaming of and hoping for?

October 25
Risking Love

Life will break you. Nobody can protect you, and living alone won't either, for solitude will break you with yearning. You have to love. You have to feel that it is the reason you are here on earth. You are here to risk your heart.

(Louise Erdrich, American author,
part Chippewa American native)

Strong medicine: "You have to love" says the author, for the struggle in life can break us down unless we realize our purpose for our being is to love. Isolation or fending off those who need us or would live with us, only asking for love and devotion in return, is senseless and self-destructive. Turn it around, ask who can, should, and are the ones I must love? They are most likely right near me. They deserve my love.

293

October 26
The Right Attitude—Indispensable

Nothing can stop the man with the right mental attitude from achieving his goal. Nothing on earth can help the man with wrong mental attitude.

(Thomas Jefferson, third president of the USA and author of *The Declaration of Independence*)

We value an education, and for knowledge, we pay a great price. But what would we pay to receive the gift of a proper mental attitude?

October 27
Courage and Determination

Living with faith and courage is something that life requires of each of us. Never give up, never give in no matter what. Fight it through, and I promise you with all my heart that God will help you.

(Kathryn Kuhlman, American evangelist)

Kathryn lived by her motto. She led Christian worship and died relatively young after extensive missions to preach the Gospel. Faith asks us to believe in God's help, and taking courage to persevere in our life's mission will earn, she believed, God's strong assistance to succeed.

October 28
Overcoming Fear

The things we fear most in organizations—fluctu-
ations, disturbances, imbalances—are the primary
sources of creativity.

(Margaret J. Wheatley, writer and
management consultant)

Recognizing that changes are constant, and inevitable parts of our lives can help us to transform our fears into hopes and positive expectations. Yes, this or that method may be "working," but a "better way to do it" is about to break down the door. Be part of the change by using the creative imagination to manage the challenges of changing times.

October 29
Direction

The only way to do great work is to love what you do. If you haven't found it yet, keep looking, don't settle.

(Steve Jobs, American business magnate, industrial designer and investor)

If you feel compelled to do your job, and it is nothing more than a source of a paycheck and a title, think about a creative change. Don't change for more money or a shorter commute. Instead, change by finding what makes you eager to get up and go to that work in the morning.

October 30
Transformation

Creativity is thinking up new things. Innovation is doing new things.

(Theodore Levitt, German American professor and economist who redirected the art of marketing)

Dr. Levitt urged companies to refocus their marketing efforts on the customers, not their internal organizations. Helping the other to find his optimum product or service? What a transformation! His creative ideas prompted constructive new campaigns. His creative ideas, tried and selected, were the catalyst for timely innovations which just worked better.

October 31
Curiosity

Curiosity about life in all its aspects, I think, is still the secret of great creative people.

(Leo Burnett, advertising executive and founder of Leo Burnett Company)

To foster curiosity, ask, "Why, how, when, by whom" when you come upon something you don't understand or would like to deeply comprehend. Who discovered gravity and how? Who developed hydraulics to transform car brakes and huge cranes? Why does a symphony enthrall the listeners? Get inside of the process. You may be that dozing creative genius who has not yet asked enough questions.

November 1
Wellness

I can feel guilty about the past, apprehensive about the future, but only in the present can I act. The ability to be in the present moment is major component of mental wellness.

(Abraham Maslow, American psychologist,
noted as the father of humanistic psychology)

The present is our time on stage. Here we have the leading role in creating our drama, our story, contributing to history. If we look too far ahead or a long way back, we are going to "flub our lines." Also, living and acting in the present is a natural state which can relieve us of excess anxieties and regrets.

November 2
Letting go

Take responsibility for your last bad decision, and let it go. Don't blame others or make excuses for yourself.

(Deepak Chopra, Indian American author
and promoter of alternative medicine)

Have you overpacked your "suitcase of worries?" Many people walk around with a backpack or suitcase full of unmanageable worries or regrets. This gradually leaves them weak or sick as a consequence of such stress. As recommended, "Let it, or them, *go!*"

November 3
Little Things

*Who can be faithful in great things if he has not
learned to be faithful in the things of daily life?*

(Dietrich Bonhoeffer, Lutheran pastor and influential theologian)

The little things are the steps to big accomplishments. When we
get up promptly and get to work energetically, we are on the way to
reach our bigger goals. When we pay close attention to the needs of
our families and coworkers, we support the team efforts of our business. Slacking off on doing the little but essential tasks undermines
progress to the greater accomplishments which we have envisioned.

November 4
Composure

We find rest in those we love, and we provide a resting place in ourselves for those who love us.

(Bernard of Clairvaux, saint and Cistercian
abbot who revitalized monasticism)

Compact and meaningful are those words of the abbot. What revitalizes us day after day so we can return to our work, reach our goals, and restore peace after conflict? St. Bernard says love. Here we regain our soul's composure and recharge our physical and emotional strength.

November 5
Resolving Things

If the past is not resolved, future relationships will suffer. Let your heart heal before you open the door to another.

(Leon Brown, pastor, master of divinity, and author)

Dwelling on the past is costly. Learning from it is economical. Pastor Brown urges carefully sorting out how and why a relationship failed before entering into a new one. Isn't this fair to both you and the new person who might be entering a special place in your life?

November 6
Consolation

There is no feeling more comforting and consoling
than knowing you are right next to the one you love.

(Oscar Wilde, Irish poet and playwright)

Refreshing, completing, and consoling are the rewarding gifts of finding and being in proximity to a true love who shares your life. As Tony Robbins (author, coach, philanthropist) reminds us, "A relationship lasts if you see it as a place you go to give, and not a place you go to take."

November 7
Gifts

You don't choose your family. They are God's gift to you as you are to them.

(Desmond Tutu, South African cleric, theologian, and human rights activist)

The first and lifelong gifts of love and family come from the ones who gave us life on this earth. The bishop reminds us that though it was not our conscious thought which brought us here, we are recipients of the great gift of life and should repay it with love and devotion as long as our parents are with us. Have you said or expressed your love and gratitude to them lately?

November 8
Momentous Actions

What can you do to promote world peace? Go home and love your family.

(Mother Teresa, saint and founder of
a religious order to help the poor)

Peace, says Mother Teresa, begins with each family. Discord, or simply a lack of love, destabilizes the family unit. Small steps like restoring love and harmony in our own family is the beginning of a greater harmony in society and essential to a world which is more at peace.

307

November 9
Centered?

> *No matter what you've done for yourself or for humanity, if you can't look back on having given love and attention to your own family, what have you really accomplished?*

(Lee Iacocca, American auto designer
and CEO of two major auto companies, Ford and Chrysler)

While many reach fame and fortune, they often look back to their beginnings and evaluate their achievements in light of their family's influences on them. And to be clear and centered in life, we must self-examine where we are and hope to become in light of our great gift of birth and upbringing. Do we appreciate that or could we be doing better at expressing love and gratitude?

November 10
Links

*In every conceivable manner, the family is (the) link
to our past and bridge to our future.*

(Alex Haley, American author of
Roots and Coast Guard veteran)

Genetics, blood type, DNA, and all that goes into our corporeal makeup stems from the gift of our parents and ancestors. What we have received is a framework for our personality and future accomplishments. But birth does not determine our outcome. Actually, it contributes a uniqueness for us to appreciate. Color, size, shape—humans come in all forms, and each one of us is tasked to make the most of his or her unique gifts by constant hard work and determination.

November 11
Visualize

> *If you look deeply into the palm of your hand, you will see your parents and all generations of your ancestors. All of them are alive in this moment. Each is present in your body. You are the continuation of each of these people.*

> (Thich Nhat Hanh, Vietnamese
> monk, and peace activist)

Poetic and deeply sensitive comments by the monk tell us to be grateful to, and reverential of, the memory of our ancestors. Looking at ourselves through this lens should make us more conscious or our gifts and consoled by the feeling of their spiritual continuation through our actions and accomplishments. They were here, they passed on, but they passed along gifts to us, and in a sense, they still walk beside us.

November 12
Constant and Consistent

Your family and your love must be cultivated like a garden. Time, effort, and imagination must be summoned constantly to keep any relationship flourishing and growing.

(Jim Rohn, entrepreneur, author, and motivational speaker)

Time, effort, and imagination are the priceless ingredients to nourish our garden of relationships. As we bring these to all who we love, family, close friends, and devoted coworkers, we will see results. And yes, the growth and blossoming will take consistent effort over the years. If you want great value, you must pay the high price.

November 13
Priorities

A man should never neglect his family for business.

(Walt Disney, American writer, film producer, creator of entertainment parks)

Make a living, but always first make a life. We hear so often that someone has succeeded at making a fortune but has gone bankrupt in the arena of family relationships. Which are the right priorities to hold before us as we begin again each week to make a living? Think about it, pray hard, then choose carefully.

November 14
Appreciation

Truly appreciate those around you, and you'll soon find many others around you. Truly appreciate life, and you'll find that you have more of it.

(Ralph Marston, soccer player and writer)

Stop by a quiet place while going to or from work and ponder the meaning of appreciating others. Who were those persons in the circle of family or friends, coworkers or teachers whose advice or lessons made a wonderful impact on you? As you go to, or return, from your work, be aware of those valuable gifts. Appreciate those givers in some tangible way. It will reward them and you. Mr. Marston also said, "What you do today can improve all your tomorrows."

November 15
Bases of Relationships

> *Relationships are based on four principles: respect,*
> *understanding, acceptance, and appreciation.*

(Mahatma Gandhi, teacher)

Complimentary appreciation is another great quality which supports relationships. Have you felt the respect of your peers? Have you enjoyed the understanding of a friend who listens intently? And have you been warmed by the understanding a parent or friend extended to you? How fortunate are those who receive all these components along with appreciation. If you have not been so blessed, maybe you might attempt to give them to others and observe the effects. Start small, continue on.

November 16
Light

There are two ways of spreading light: to be the candle or the mirror that reflects it.

(Edith Wharton, novelist, short-
story writer, and designer)

What if presently, you are not the sun that shines, the star that guides, or the candle that gives warm light? As Ms. Wharton advises, be at least a reflector of the light you find in others. Replicate their graciousness or brilliance by imitating the best you find in their lives. Eventually, your own light will illuminate the path for others to follow.

November 17
Leaders

> *If your actions inspire others to dream more, learn more, do more, and become more, you are a leader.*

(John Quincy Adams, statesman and
sixth president of the USA)

More than reflecting light and power, your own actions in whatever positive manner, they influence others will bring out in them progress on the road to progress and fulfillment. In many small ways, you are exercising leadership.

November 18
Happiness

Remember that there is no happiness in having or in getting but only in giving. Reach out. Share. Smile. Hug. Happiness is a perfume you cannot share without getting a few drops on yourself.

(Augustine "Og" Mandino, American
self-help and inspirational author)

Mr. Mandino said that true happiness lies within us. But instead of a possession, it is a dynamic born of giving to others. Going outside of yourself to lift up or help heal other people, by words and embraces, contributes to their lives and immediately nourishes our own psyche. Happiness is not a thing to hoard but a lifelong career of helping others reach fulfillment.

November 19
Key Contributor

> *If you could only sense how important you are to the*
> *lives of those you meet, how important you can be*
> *to the people you may never even dream of. There is*
> *something of yourself that you leave at every meeting*
> *with another person.*

> (Fred Rogers, minister, TV personality and
> producer of *Mr. Rogers' Neighborhood*)

Directly or indirectly, our touch may be so transformative that it directs or redirects an individual or group of people in an essential way. We meet, speak with, or simply nod to so many on our way to and from our tasks. Think about the person to whom you simply offered to give a seat on a bus or train or the people you mentor or the child you helped understand that knotty homework problem. Life goes on, as we may hardly notice the light in their eyes, but their "hearts have been touched."

November 20
Positive Change

Every small positive change we make in ourselves repays us in confidence in the future.

(Alice Walker, American poet, novelist, writer of *The Color Purple*)

Can we think of positive change as a "deposit" into our confidence bank account? When we overcome inertia and go off in a positive direction, the motion continues onward. We are growing stronger in the habit of positivity versus negativity. A result: more strength and trust in our ability to do and become better.

November 21
Grateful

To be grateful is to recognize the love of God in everything.

(Thomas Merton, Trappist monk,
theologian, writer, and mystic)

All creation explains the genius and care of God who designed us and the marvelous planet which is our home. Thoughts and acts of gratitude are acknowledging the goodness and love which God has implanted in nature and the wonderful complexity of ourselves and our neighbors. All are God's handwriting. As Monsignor Fulton J. Sheen, Catholic priest, once wrote about this, "God writes his name on the soul of every man."

November 22
Occasions

When you rise in the morning, give thanks for the light, for your life, for your strength. Give thanks for your food and for the joy of living. If you see no reason to give thanks, the fault lies in yourself.

(Tecumseh, Shawnee American Indian leader)

How can we fail to rise to these occasions which prompt feelings of gratitude? Is our day so full of concerns, anxieties, or multiple to-do lists that we become oblivious to the wonders of our existence, strengths, and what nourishes us? Stop and look around as did a man of action. Without books or expensive education, his natural wisdom speaks to us.

November 23
A Good Heart

*O Lord that lends me a life, lend me a heart replete
with thankfulness.*

(William Shakespeare, outstanding playwright, poet, and actor)

One of the greatest writers and dramatists, William Shakespeare utters a simple but profound prayer for the great gift of life. Each of us here and now has this gift of life, an existence of innumerable possible creative actions. We may not surpass "The Bard of Avon," but in our lifelong drama, our hearts should beat "replete with thankfulness."

November 24
Purposeful

> *The proper function of man is to live, not to exist. I*
> *shall not waste my days in trying to prolong them. I*
> *shall use my time.*

(Jack London, born John Griffith
Chaney, novelist, poet and activist)

Whatever amount of time is granted or lent to us, quality of life surpasses mere quantity. Another writer, William Faulkner, said, "I believe that man will not merely endure, he will prevail." It seems that we are placed here not merely to survive but to thrive.

November 25
Responsibility

> *If you take responsibility for yourself, you will*
> *develop a hunger to accomplish your dreams.*

(Les Brown, former US congress-
man and motivational speaker)

Where does the fire come from when we do not feel the urge to continue our work or even begin a new project? Mr. Brown points out that we need to acquire a sense of self-responsibility which engages our desire or hunger to get on with purpose and drive to the goal.

November 26
Good News!

> *Everyone has inside of him a piece of good news. The good news is that you don't know how great you can be! How much you can love! What you can accomplish! And what your potential is!*

> (Anne Frank, a young German Dutch
> girl who composed her famous
> diary during World War II)

For a young woman living in hiding and in fear of being exiled and executed during the Holocaust of WW II, Anne lifted her spirits and ours by focusing on the immense potential for good within each of us. She was an extraordinary, brave soul who can inspire us even on the darkest of our days.

November 27
Thanksgiving

*No matter what our circumstance, we can find a
reason to be thankful.*

(Melody Beattie, American
author of self-help books)

In the USA, November's last Thursday of the month is dedi-
cated to give thanks to God and celebrate our blessings. Whether we
gather with family and friends to share our table and recall our blessings or struggle to find reasons to be grateful, it's a time to reflect.
Some must think hard to find the blessings in their lives, but as Ms.
Beattie asserts, we can and must find them and be thankful for them.

November 28
Practice

A basic law: The more you practice the art of thankfulness, the more you have to be thankful for.

(Norman Vincent Peale, pastor and self-help book author)

When you think about this, you can compare it to a "compounding effect." Your positive attitude of gratitude for people, things, and mere existence provokes a multiplying effect. The more you see the good in life, the stronger you are and can reach out with positivity to others.

November 29
Spreading Knowledge

> *The best thing a human being can do is to help another human being know more.*

(Charlie Munger, American investor, philanthropist, and designer)

What can we share or give away and still possess? Is it some important knowledge or insights which we have found helpful and perduring in their value? We know what we know but are often hurt by proceeding into the unknown pitfalls ahead of us. If you can wisely advise someone to plan for his or her future success in matters of relationships, careers, or financial planning, do so. What have you lost? Nothing. And what was gained? Possibly an immense value for another and a satisfaction that you helped.

November 30
Value

Knowledge is of no value unless you put it into practice.

(Anton Chekhov, Russian playwright and short story writer)

Mr. Munger advocates the sharing of knowledge, and Mr. Chekhov tells us that the opposite, the hoarding of knowledge, is selfish and unproductive. Why keep such treasure to yourself? Would you buy a great deal of perishable fruit and let it spoil uneaten or shared? Sounds unreasonable, doesn't it?

December 1
Treasure

> *Knowledge is happiness to know the thoughts and deeds that have marked man's progress is to feel the great heartthrobs of humanity through the centuries. And if one does not feel in these pulsations a heavenward striving, one must be deaf to the harmonies of life.*

(Helen Keller, American author, activist
for the visually impaired, and lecturer)

If Helen Keller overcame her blindness and being deaf, earned a bachelor's degree, and helped countless others, what is holding us back from appreciating our potential? Which sources of information, knowledge, and training are not available to us in our modern world? Look around, learn, and share all we can with all who are open to this treasure.

December 2
Growth

The mind, once stretched by a new idea, never returns to its original dimensions.

(Ralph Waldo Emerson, American
poet, philosopher and essayist)

Physical growth has its limits, but intelligence and appreciation of new ideas, music, art, and theology seem to expand us without limits. Being open to learning, sharing that treasure, and helping as much as possible can keep a smile on your face in good or bad times.

December 3
Attainment

To know the will of God is the greatest knowledge!
To do the will of God is the greatest achievement.

(George W. Truett, pastor of the First Baptist
Church in Dallas, Texas, author, and president of the Southern Baptist Convention)

Echoing St. Augustine, this pastor rose from very humble beginnings to reach prominence in education and administration. Every
day, we begin our tasks, and we try to reach out desired achievements
and attain our goals. But let's remember that the will of our Creator
is paramount. The Scriptures tell us in summary, "Love God with
your whole heart and soul, and your neighbor as yourself." As Pastor
Truett reminds us, doing the will of God is our greatest achievement.

December 4
Significance

Don't ever allow yourself to feel trapped by your choices. Take a look at yourself. You are a unique person created for a specific purpose. Your gifts matter. Your dreams matter. You matter.

(Michael Oher, professional football player who overcame poverty and a broken family to reach success)

A child from a broken family, neglected, and finally adopted, educated, and a competitive athlete, Mr. Oher personifies the truth of his assertions. He was left by the roadside, but with the love, the help of others, and his developed athletic skills, he achieved success. A film, *The Blind Side*, portrays his life story.

Control or Controlled?

> *Don't allow your past or present condition to control you. It's just a process that you're going through to get you to the next level.*

(Thomas Dexter Jakes, known as T. D. Jakes, bishop, author and filmmaker)

Life events can uplift us, detour us, or flatten us. But our outcome is not ruled by external events but rather our interpretation of what these events can mean for us and how they can be treated either as "stumbling stones or building blocks." Recall the life of Michael Oher and his adoptive family. There is a story of controlling life, finding a "survive and thrive" attitude.

December 5
Worry Not

Worry does not empty tomorrow of its sorrow. It empties today of its strength.

(Corrie ten Boom, Dutch watchmaker and author, who, together with her family, saved Jewish people from the Holocaust during World War II)

Biblical beliefs motivated a crusade to spare her Jewish Neighbors who were destined for extermination. Corrie was strong, fearless, and lived out her belief that hope conquers fear. As she also said, "Never be afraid to trust an unknown future to a known God."

335

Getting On with It

> *No matter how you feel, get up, dress up, show up,*
> *and never give up.*

(Australian proverb)

The spirit of the "can-do" Aussie—If everyone had that attitude and practiced that program, there would be layoffs at the offices of unemployment

December 6
The Impossible (Eventually Accomplished)

It always seems impossible until it's done.

(Australian proverb)

From Leonardo da Vinci's sketches of helicopters to actual medical rescue helicopters, people often say, "It cannot be done," and then sooner or later, most of it *is* done. Maybe as we contemplate the unlikely, we should reset our thinking to a "How can it be done?" instead of stating it "never can be done."

December 7
Efforts (Pull and Steer)

We cannot control the wind, but we can direct the sail.

(Australian proverb)

To get to where we want to be, the winds may oppose our ship. The value of a headwind is that we can sail obliquely to the wind and still arrive at our destination. Sailing requires pulling on the ropes and tugging at the rudder. All of life requires appropriate efforts to succeed. And another idea:

Getting on with It

Remember, no matter how you feel, get up, dress up, show up, and never give up.

(Australian proverb)

This is the spirit of the "can-do" Aussie.

December 8
Dreams

Dreams are our realities in waiting. In dreams, we plant the seeds of our future.

(Australian proverb)

As the dreamers who lived before us, thought of humans flying through the sky, or astronauts traveling in outer space, the accomplishments came along later and then, sooner and sooner. Dream, write, draw, communicate. One day, your far-fetched dream may take us there.

December 9
Time

Never give up on a dream just because of the time it will take to accomplish it. The time will pass anyway.

(Earl Nightingale, American author, broad-caster, and speaker on human development)

Time is the measurement of motions, like our planet's journey around the sun is completed in what we call 365 days. A woman, fifty years old, dreamed of becoming a doctor and was told, "You will spend five years and be fifty-five when you graduate." She acknowledged that but replied, "If I don't go to medical school, in five years I will be fifty-five anyway and still be without my medical degree." What are you choosing to do or not do in the next one, two, or five years? It could make an enormous difference in your future.

December 10
Determined or Free?

*Life is like a game of cards. The hand you are dealt
is determinism, the way you play it is free will.*

(Jawaharlal Nehru, independence leader
and first prime minister of India)

Freedom is an inborn desire in all human beings. Defy determinism and embrace our freedom. From it comes the opportunities to be creative and benefit our society. In every small way, we can be good leaders. We do that within our families, schools, and companies by teamwork and contributing to one another. Some lead millions to freedom, but each individual must play a part in that progression.

December 11
Victory

If I can overcome myself today, I'll be able to attain
victory tomorrow.

(Japanese proverb)

What's standing in our way of winning is usually our own lack of will power to begin and persevere in a hard task. Whether we promise to exercise or eat right or study more, tomorrow, the task unbegun is likely never done. An old adage is "Well begun is half done" and tells us that the Japanese proverb contains an efficient formula. Overcome inertia or even loathing for the job, and you conquer your biggest obstacle. As mentioned near the beginning of this yearlong journey, "Do it now! Don't procrastinate."

December 12
Capacity

If you are filled with pride, then you will have no room for wisdom.

(African proverb)

At times we think we know it all. And usually, we are shocked to discover there are some things we just "missed or overlooked." Socrates declared, "I know that I know nothing," and by that shocking overstatement, sent us looking for the truth. What is our capacity for wisdom? Do we respect the thoughts of others or look for evidence which might contradict our estimations or deeply held theories? A cup filled with flour has little capacity for a hot cup of tea.

December 13
Humility

> *When you educate a man, you educate an individual. When you educate a woman, you educate a generation.*

> (African proverb)

About half of the world population is male and the other female. If the saying is correct, that women will bring their wisdom downstream to their children and grandchildren, then the men in the other half of the population should be humbled. Certainly, it's time for them to put attention and effort into the effective education of their children. In doing that, they can start catching up to the better educators among us.

December 14
Value

> *Hold a true friend with both hands.*

(African proverb)

So many pitfalls caused by our pride, so many threats hiding around corners due to our recklessness, and so many safeguards provided by true friends—As the proverb recommends, we should seek out and strongly bond to good and loyal friends. They see our unseen weaknesses, and detect our hidden strengths. Call or visit your true friend often.

December 15
Survival

In youth, we learn. In old age, we understand.

(Ecuadorian proverb)

He who hears no advice will not reach old age.

(Bolivian proverb)

In our early years, we absorb so many facts and weave them into information and knowledge. But take time to relate various points of knowledge into understanding of ourselves and our world. Being limited, we still need the guidance of true friends, and pastors to help us to survive for the long journey onward until we become grandparents and great-grandparents. Decades of survival requires help from all sides.

December 16
A Lesson

> A Cherokee Elder tells a boy, "There are two wolves fighting within me, one is bad. He is filled with anger, envy, sorrow, regret, greed, arrogance, self-pity, lies, false pride, superiority, and self-doubt. The other is good. He is joy, peace, love, hope, serenity, humility, kindness, benevolence, empathy, generosity, truth, compassion, and faith." The elder says, "The same fight is going on inside of you and everyone else.
>
> The boy asks, "Which wolf will win?"
>
> The elder replied, "The one you feed."

American natives knew how to live well and mostly avoid conflicts with neighboring tribes. But this story illustrated how the most terrible conflicts are the ones within us. Winning over our "bad wolf" requires "staving him out," or defeating our brutish selfish desires which corrode our souls. Feeding the "good wolf" is the opposite task. And the more we go out to serve our fellow man, the stronger the "good wolf" will become.

December 17
A Blessing

May the sun bring you new energy by day. May the moon softly restore you by night. May the rain wash away your worries. May the breeze blow new strength into your being. May you walk gently through the world and know its beauty all the days of your life.

(Apache Blessing)

A catalog of blessings which would make a life most happy and content—what a wise and kind list has this American native of the Apache tribe left to us. Certainly, this is a marvelous "wish list" to offer anyone who needs encouragement or consolation.

December 18
Serve and Protect

The warrior's task is to take care of the elderly, the defenseless, those who cannot provide for themselves, and above all, the children, the future of humanity.

(Sitting Bull, Hunkpapa and Lakota
Indian, spiritual and military leader)

Warriors fight for the survival of the tribe or nation. But Sitting Bull reminds us that the most noble task of the brave is to care for the most needy.

December 19
Healing

May the stars carry your sadness away. May the flowers fill your heart with beauty. May hope forever wipe away your tears. And above all, may silence make you strong.

(Chief Dan George, American Indian, a chief of the Tsleil-Waututh Nation, author, and screen actor)

The chief shares some Native American wisdom to look up, look around, and then, seeing the stars and the beauty of nature, we can heal. Learning to be "still" grants us the power of internal strength and endurance.

December 20
Humility

> *Let us walk softly on the earth with all living beings,*
> *great and small, remembering as we go that one*
> *God, kind and wise, created all.*

(American Native saying)

Respect for our land, water, and resources should make us considerate of the gift of our Planet and its wonderful creatures. Man and all other creatures were created by a wise and kind God, and our job is to be good stewards of all these riches. Invest in, but do not destroy or defile, our treasures.

December 21
Environment

All things are connected. Whatever befalls the earth,
befalls the sons of the earth.

(Chief Seattle, Squamish American Indian)

The chief, like many of the Native Americans who lived across the North American continent, were wise in their outlook and concern for the earth which provided, food, water, and all they needed for life. Today we are again trying to strike a balance between taking and guarding the rich resources of our land and waters. Those early peoples had exemplary great respect and courage. The chief also offered this wisdom, "There is no death, only a change of worlds."

December 22
A Good Heart

*Above all else, guard your heart, for everything you
do flows from it.* (Proverbs 4:23)

American Indian wisdom promotes love for the pure and generous life. Biblical Wisdom likewise reminds us to be pure in spirit and that our heart is like the headwaters of a great river. Clean water nourishes everything in its path. Make our hearts clean and purposeful, and we will protect everyone and everything with kind and generous actions as we go through life.

December 23
Look Up to God

For the Lord gives wisdom; from His mouth come knowledge and understanding. (Proverbs 2:6)

Our life is brief, even in terms of eighty or one hundred years on this earth, we live and learn slowly. We give what we can and hope to pass along something of value to our family, friends, and community. But how can we obtain real knowledge, understanding, and wisdom without the source of everything that is good, true, and beautiful— God the Creator. Recall the humility of the Native Americans and their respect for the Great Spirit as they saw God. Recall how they understood the battle for the soul of man and wanted to feed the good "wolf" inside. Turn to the Lord and ask for help.

Ask and it will be given to you. Seek and you will find. Knock and the door will be opened to you. (Matthew 7:7)

December 24
Trust

> *Trust in the Lord with all your heart and lean not on your own understanding. In all your ways, acknowledge Him, and He shall direct your paths.* (Proverbs 3:5–6)

Who can we trust? In whom should we place our faith and follow? As we find out so often, the human leaders or celebrities who dazzle us with programs, slogans, or manifestoes are proven wrong. The Scripture advises turning to the best counselor we can have, the Lord. The proud are often deluded by their self-adoration. The humble are more prepared to accept what is true and good. From the shepherds who followed the Christmas "glad tidings" and went to Bethlehem to the Native Americans who revered the "Great Spirit," we can look to the Lord for the best directions in life.

December 25
A Star

Star of wonder, star of night, guide us to that perfect light.

(Lines from the Christmas Carol, "We
Three Kings of Orient Are.")

In late winter, we celebrate the birth of Jesus of Nazareth. For many believers, He is acknowledged as the Son of God who came to us in human form some two thousand years ago to teach us and return us to God's adopted family once more. Many wonders from His birth to His miracles, confirm His identity and His role in our path to a reward with God after this life. Whether you are a believer or a nonbeliever, His teachings are worthy of imitation. He guides us in all the right ways of love and service. His teachings are the completion of precepts in the Old Testament and invite all men beyond Israelites to follow Him.

December 26
Fulfillment

If God is all you have, you have all you need. (John 14:18)

God our Creator and final destiny is our beginning and our final goal. So many words from all over the globe and down through the ages have asked the questions, "Why are we here? What must we do? How can we avoid failure? When will we find fulfillment?" In his concise and precise words, Saint John tells us God is the answer. He is all you require. And His answers to those questions flow from Scripture, the prophets, and all whose divinely inspired words which come down to us by recorded oral or written history. Search, find, and follow them, and you will feed the good power in you.

December 27
A Great Teaching

> *And he answering said, "Thou shalt love the Lord*
> *thy God with all they heart and all thy soul and all*
> *thy strength and with all thy mind and thy neighbor*
> *as thyself.* (Luke 10:27)

From Jesus, the great teacher comes the distillation of all the laws of the Old and New Testament. Love God without boundaries, and then your fellow man as much as yourself. Simple, comprehensive, and an enormous task. Who can supply the help we need to fulfill this task? God invites us to ask for all the help we need. "Ask and you shall receive."

December 28
Great and Greatest

And now abide faith, hope, love, these three; but the greatest of these is love. (1 Corinthians 13:13)

Love is patient, love is kind. It does not envy, it does not boast, it is not proud. It is not rude, it is not self-seeking, it is not easily angered, it keeps no record of wrongs. Love does not delight in evil but rejoices in the truth. (1 Corinthians 13:4–7)

And what is this love commanded by God? First, we hear from St. Paul that of the three great virtues of faith, hope, and charity, the last which is love is the greatest virtue. Love is the extension of our goodwill and actions to others. It exists in its best form as St. Paul says—kind, disciplined, humble, and honest. If you ever felt the joy of doing something appropriate and good for someone without expectation of praise or reward, you have extended that which is really love to another.

December 29
Perseverance

Grant me, O Lord my God, a mind to know You, a heart to seek You, wisdom to find You, faithful perseverance in waiting for You, and hope of finally embracing you.

(St. Thomas Aquinas, Italian Dominican
priest, doctor of the church)

Finding what to do, embracing a life of service as the expression of love, and enduring to the end is what St. Thomas prayed for, when we attempt to be our best selves, we need help in all of these dimensions. Prayer is communicating with God. Sometimes we ask, sometimes we thank, often we question. It is all part of a good conversation with the supreme listener!

December 30
Peace Within

May today there be peace within. May you trust that you are exactly where you are meant to be. May you not forget the infinite possibilities that are born of faith in yourself and others. May you use the gifts that you have received and pass on the love that has been given to you.

(St. Therese of Lisieux, Carmelite
nun and author)

But when you look around at your life and progression toward becoming your best self, you might wonder, *Where am I?* And as Saint Therese who was attuned to God posits this reply, "Trust that you are exactly where you are meant to be." At a beginning, a middle point, or nearing the end of life, you are still in the right place as you strive to be your best. Persevere! St. Therese wrote this note of caution to us, "The world is thy ship and not thy home."

December 31
Visitors All

> *We are all visitors to this time, this place. We are just*
> *passing through. Our purpose here is to observe, to*
> *learn, to grow, to love, and then we return home.*

(Australian aboriginal proverb)

The journey on this earth is designed to help us become what God intends us to be. The Greeks called this "entelechy" or fulfillment of our inner potential. Live, learn, love, grow, and become what the divine artist sketched out for each of us to be.

Afterword

May any words, which you have read and pondered here, be a help to you as you make your way through life, trying to become your "best self."

About the Author

 The author, born in Brooklyn, New York, was raised by a loving and generous family who instilled in him a love of educating and caring for others. Following twin careers in education and medical equipment sales, he retired to volunteer work and a Project "EMI," selected quotes and comments to *educate, motivate,* and *inspire.*

Comments:

It has been a pleasure waking up with your motivational quotes. I feel armed for the day, with mantra-level confidence to succeed in my day.

—Austin Vitaliano
Operatic Tenor

Wisdom for Millennials motivates us to action by inculcating in us solid virtues for achieving right attitudes of mind and soul.

—Frank Heelan, EdD
Retired School Superintendent
Edison, New Jersey

A quick and wonderful read to take anywhere—great for meditation and reflection, recommended to all who seek peace, guidance, and tranquility.

—Emily Wehner
Retired Teacher
Oakland Gardens, New York

For the person looking for a way to find a better life, this book can offer a compass that points in that direction.

—Andrew Ferdinandi, PhD
St. John's University
Bayside, New York

CPSIA information can be obtained
at www.ICGtesting.com
Printed in the USA
LVHW112129140722
723579LV00019B/136

9 781639 611584